A Guide to New Jersey Craft Breweries

South Jersey Edition

2017-2018

Maureen Fitzpatrick

Photographs by Joan Stoltzfus

Printed in the United States

ISBN 10: 0-9993959-0-4
ISBN 13: 978-0-9993959-05

DEDICATION

Dedicated to those who make great beer...thank you!

Contents

Acknowledgements

Thank you to all the brewery owners and brewers who helped make this book possible, especially those who straightened us out on some of the beer terminology.

Thank you to the following people who took the time to point out misplaced commas, dropped words, and all the other writing errors that happened after spending days affixed to the computer with little sleep. They are Lynn Wyrovsky, Mary Kate Fitzpatrick, Molly Fitzpatrick, Meghan Deutsch, and Kathryn Drewes.

Also thank you to the following people who suffered through many an uncooked dinner while we were busy traveling around tasting beer: John Fitzpatrick, Erin Fitzpatrick, Josh Fitzpatrick, Aidan Fitzpatrick, and Andrew Stoltzfus.

Thank you *Visit South Jersey* for graciously adding a piece to the book. They are an invaluable source for things to do in South Jersey. Please visit them at www.visitsouthjersey.com.

Are you ready to drink some craft beer?

Introduction

Ahhhh, the feel of a cold beer swimming in your mouth as it makes its way down your parched throat. There is nothing like the experience of ending a long work day with an ice cold beer. Somehow, that first sip grabs hold of the stress and expels it from our souls. And thanks to an uptick in craft breweries, our choices of style and brand have made many "of drinking age" humans feel like kids in a candy store.

In a time where words like malt, hops, yeast, and barley have turned many a basic man into a beer snob, it's no longer uncool to have a distinguished vocabulary. Enter any craft brewery and you'll hear such sophisticated phrases as, "This beer has a nose of... " and " The mouthfeel is creamy and the finish is smooth..." And yes, there are even some very manly men using the word "bouquet" to describe the aroma or smell of the beer. Amazing what a beverage can do.

If you haven't yet hopped on the craft brewery train, it's time you do. You will discover a wonderful world of beer you never knew existed, and we are here to help. Enjoy the following guide. You will get a brief introduction to the breweries and important information to help you decide when and where to go. Then check out our suggestions for beer trails. What better way to spend the day than tasting a variety of the finest brews in South Jersey and meeting some great people.

Beer fact: Beer shines copper!

Helpful Beer Terminology

Ale: Beer fermented at warmer temperatures using top fermenting yeast.

ABV: Alcohol by volume

Cask: Container for holding beer, barrel shaped. Cask beer is unfiltered and served from the cask. Tends to have less carbonation and more complex flavor.

Craft beer: Traditional style beer brewed at small independent breweries, often using a twist of innovation and a dash of imagination.

Hops: Vine yielding small pinecone like flowers, used to flavor the beer. They add bitterness and aroma. Adding hops in different parts of the brewing process produces different flavors.

IPA: India Pale Ale, hoppy.

Lager: Beer fermented at colder temperatures using bottom fermenting yeast. Produces a crisp beer. Originates from Czech Republic, formally the Austrian Empire.

Mash: Mixture of water and malt which makes the wort, the strained liquid which contains the grain sugars.

Mouthfeel: How the beer feels in the mouth.

Pale Ale: Hop forward ale brewed with a pale malt resulting in a golden color.

Porter: Darker beer, tends to be more bitter, brewed with brown malt.

Saison: Mixture of carbonated pale ale and sometimes something fruity. Might have a spicy bite.

Session beer: Has less of an alcohol content.

Stout: Dark beer made with roasted grains, tend to be thicker and stronger.

Tripel: Strong pale ale.

Important Information: Breweries that are **nearing completion** at the time of this publication are noted with an **asterisk *** Please check their web or social media sites to ensure that they are open.

All the information in this book is up-to-date as of publication. We are not responsible if a brewery changes days, hours, beer selection, etc.

Please drink responsibly. Always assign a designated driver. We have beer trails to follow in this book. We want you to enjoy them, but please take Uber, Lyft, taxi, or assign a driver. We can't be responsible for poor choices.

New breweries are always popping up like fragrant flowers. If you are opening one or know of one opening in South Jersey, let us know about it. We will put it in the next edition! Contact information is in back of book.

Remember, craft breweries are not allowed to serve food per NJ law. Bring your own or have it delivered in from a surrounding restaurant.

Atlantic County

Atlantic County Beer Trail Map

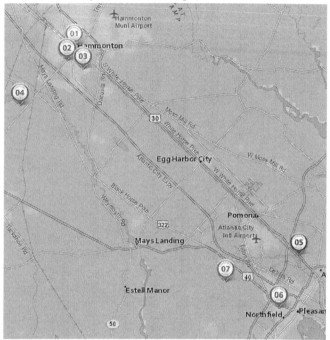

1)Three 3's 2)Tomfoolery 3)Vinyl 4)Black
Horse 5)Garden State 6)Hidden Sands
7)Tuckahoe

Beer trail one: Start at Three 3's. *Taste beer.*
Walk around the corner to Tomfoolery. *Taste
beer.* Drive or walk half mile down Washington
Street to Vinyl. *Taste beer.* Drive seven minutes
via 12th Street and the Black Horse Pike to Black
Horse Brewery (Check if opened) *Taste beer.*

Beer trail two: Start at Garden State. *Taste*

beer. Drive nine minutes via Garden State Parkway to Hidden Sands. (Check if open) *Taste beer.* Drive eight minutes via Route 40 and Washington Ave to Tuckahoe. *Taste Beer.*

Fun Fact: Cenosillicaphobia is the fear of an empty beer glass.

*Black Horse Brewery (opening late 2017 – early 2018)

Joe Walker and Howard Zane decided to open their craft brewery, **Black Horse Brewery,** during a moment, or many moments of what Joe himself calls, "*insanity.*" Partners in a machine shop that has been in business for over fifty years, the two decided to take their good business relationship to new levels.

The brewery will be located in the building attached to the machine shop at 18 East Black Horse Pike in Folsom, NJ. Expect a nouveau industrial vibe mixed with machining history.

Black Horse Brewery will produce traditional, well balanced beers with plenty of specialty styles only available at the brewery's tasting room. They will brew with a unique twist too. **Black Horse Brewery** will put added attention on their yeast strains and fermentation procedures. This will produce one- of-a- kind beers, ready to please your palate.

Black Horse Brewery looks forward to welcoming you!

Important Information:

Address: 18 East Black Horse Pike, Williamstown, NJ 08094

Phone: (609)561-9323

Website: www.blackhorsebrewerynj.com

Email: brewer@blackhorsebrewerynj.com

Days and hours: Check website

Social media:

https://www.facebook.com/Black-Horse-Brewery-248135522288184/

https://instagram.com/blackhorsebrewery_nj

Ask twelve brewers a question and you will get thirteen answers.

Garden State Beer Company

Garden State Beer Company

If you are driving down Route 30 in Galloway, you might be heading to the shore. Though the shore is a great place to go, there is a better destination in which to head; one which will refresh you, invigorate your senses, cool you off on a hot summer day, and warm you up on a cool evening. **Garden State Beer Company** is a gem of a find located in the old *Deloretos Night Club*. After searching for a location for four years, this former hot spot "found" its owners Jason Stairs, his wife, Carisa, Brian Krenzien, and Bryan Saul.

Jason, an explosives chemist -*yes, you read that right*- wanted to do more with his PhD in chemistry. Sitting in meetings and answering emails did not scratch his itch to create and tinker in a lab. Being a thoughtful husband, Jason asked Carisa, also a chemist, if he could use his free time to make fireworks. After a very firm, "**No**," Jason and Carisa agreed a brewery would give them the opportunity to use their chemistry backgrounds, allow them some hands-on creativity, and become an enjoyable family business.

After sandblasting glittery black paint off the stone walls, pulling up stained and filthy carpet, and fixing nine years worth of decay, a bright and airy brewery emerged. **Garden State** boasts a long bar, plenty of seating for guests or special events, and even a gathering area for children to watch television and play. What's more, **Garden State** comes with its very own ghost. On the first anniversary of the opening, the brewery's motion detector went off multiple times. When Jason went to investigate in the basement, music was playing from an *unplugged* ice hockey game. In awe of what he was experiencing, he called the rest of the family down to witness. *Ta-da-da-da-DA*! The music ended just in time for the family to see and record the incident. However, upon looking for the video on the phone, it was nowhere to be found. Spooky, but so cool!

Aside from their special ghost, **Garden State Beer Company** has beers that the average, everyday person can enjoy. While they offer the hoppier, more robust beers, such as ***Nucky's Empirial IPA,*** there are plenty of fresh, handcrafted, easy drinking beers, like their most popular ***Blue Jersey American Wheat***, a drinkable, balanced beer, and their ***Cream of the***

Crop, styled similar to an American standard lager.

Knowing more than a bit about science, Jason makes sure the water chemistry is closely controlled to produce the very best tasting beer. He succeeds. The beers are surefire hits and you will absolutely find one you love.

Be sure to stop at this family owned, family friendly brewery. Maybe you'll be lucky and make a new friend...or an invisible one.

Important Information:

Address: 247 East White Horse Pike, Galloway, NJ 08205

Phone: (609)232-2337

Website: http://www.gardenstatebeerco.com

Email: info@gardenstatebeerco.com

Days and hours: Wed-Sat 12-9, Sun 12-5

To go: growlers, kegs

Events: Thursday music, Friday quizzo, yoga, paint and pints, various benefits (check social media)

Social media:

https://www.facebook.com/GardenStateBeerCo

http://instagram/gardenstatebeerco

Twitter@gardenstatebco

Matt Helm from Hidden Sands discusses the brew system.

*Hidden Sands Brewing Company (opening Fall 2017)

Welcome to **Hidden Sands Brewing Company**, a 7,500 square foot brewery boasting over 2,700 feet of multi-level tasting rooms. When you get three successful businessmen together, all with a penchant for good beer and quality ingredients, the rest of us benefit. And benefit we do with the opening of this excellence driven, craft brewery located in Egg Harbor Township, NJ. Using top quality water and a seasoned brewer, **Hidden Sands** produces some of the finest beer around.

Deep in the earth underneath this brewery, lays an aquifer known as 800-foot Sands. The water from this aquifer is what brilliant beer is brewed from. This water holds the perfect mineral content to create beer to knock your socks off. Superb water, easy access to major roads and Atlantic City, fresh local ingredients, and a familiar building, collaborate to make the location of **Hidden Sands** the perfect place for this automated microbrewery. Matt Helm, Tony Cepparulo, and John Cipriani, CPA, came together with one goal in mind...create a brewery that allows the public to relax in a fun space, drinking the very best beer. This brewery is the perfect spot for a party, meeting, business happy hour, or a family friendly break from the hot sun of the shore.

Hidden Sands is quite unique in its brewing process. It uses a state-of-the-art brewing system complete with a Siemens Braumat Compact, a process logic board that keeps each recipe consistent and delicious. With many years between them in the restaurant industry, both Matt and Tony know the importance of delivering consistently delicious products, pleasing the consumer to encourage return business, and sending them home with a smile. The beers here are consumer driven and attention to detail will never be cut. A quality control lab makes sure that each and every pint poured will have been brewed to perfection.

Hidden Sands is proud to announce its flagship beers: ***Sandy Ale***, a culinary pale ale; ***First Drop***, a breakfast style Baltic porter; ***Pump Handle***, a honey wheat ale; and their ***Unfathomable Depths IPA series***, each IPA named after depth samples taken while drilling the well. You are sure to find one or many to suit your taste.

Relax in the mezzanine or the lower tasting room, take in the view of the expansive brew area from the upper level, sip on a beer made from the best water possible, and entertain yourself, colleagues, and friends in this brand new craft brewery, **Hidden Sands Brewing Company.** It will certainly become your favorite shore retreat.

Important Information:

Address: 6754 Washington Ave. Unit B, Egg Harbor Township, NJ 08234

Phone: (609)910-2009

Website: www.hiddensands.com

Email: matthelm@hiddensands.com

Days and hours: Check website, though 7 days is the goal

To go: growlers, crowlers, cans planned, package goods

Events: Many planned, such as festivals in the back lot, please check website for events

Social media:
https://www.facebook.com/hiddensandsbeer

https://www.instagram.com/hiddensandsbeer

Twitter@HiddenSandsBeer

-Graphic courtesy of Hidden Sands

Three 3's in Hammonton.

Three 3's Brewing Company

When you pull into 50 13th Street in Hammonton, NJ, you'll first notice a sign on the brick exterior of this repository style building. Three fingers, reminiscent of a child learning his numbers, greets you along with a name, **Three 3's Brewing Co**. The name has an interesting history. **Three 3's** is home to what was once a local printing company whose address was 333 Washington Street. Turned into a craft brewery in 2016, **Three 3's** has breathed liquid life into the old space.

Three 3's Brewing Co. was founded by a local beer enthusiast turned head brewer. What better retirement project than starting a craft brewery! The success of the brewery led him to enlist the help of the Geller family who assist with the day-to-day operations. Everyone works as a team to continue brewing better beer, with a strong focus on quality. In this brewery, no one is more important than the other. "We all work as a team and play an equally important role," is Mike Geller's humble statement. Mike, his family, and his colleagues aim to continue innovating new beers and bring them to the public. With its focus on IPAs, all made in full size batches, this brewery distributes its impressive beers to all areas of NJ, in addition to hosting a fun tasting room alive with camaraderie. For those less inclined to a good IPA, **Three 3's** offers saisons in the summer and stouts and porters in the fall and winter. While visiting, try the popular *Drenched IPA* with its notes of peach, mango and citrus; or try the *Kaos*, a brewery favorite. With twelve beers on tap, and a rotating schedule, there's always something new to savor.

This brewery is quite unique in that it uses unitanks, rather than the more popular brite tanks. The unitanks allow for the beer making process to occur in one location as both a fermenter and an aging tank. A new pilot system will give ground to new flavors, soon to bless your taste buds.

Three 3's Brewing Company has become a local favorite, even for area pets. The spent grain is sent to farmers and also used to make dog treats, available for pets that visit the tasting room or to bring home to pup. **Three 3's** is also a big advocate of using local ingredients. Any fruit used in their beer is grown at local farms, keeping community in their values and their products.

   Stop by and sit at a long, family style table, where you may be asked by a kind patron to share a pizza from a local restaurant; or relax on the cozy corner couch and take a breather. A few things here are definite: fellowship and beer are paramount and making a new friend a certainty. Stop on in.

Important Information:

 Address: 50 13th Street, Hammonton, NJ 08037

Phone: (732)814-1396

Website: www.three3sbrewing.com

Email: three3sbrewing@gmail.com

Days and Hours: Wed-Thurs 5-8, Fri 3-9, Sat 1-9, Sun 12-6

To go: growlers, kegs

Events: 5K on last Sunday of every month

Social media:

www.facebook.com/Three3sbrewing/

www.instagram.com/three3sbrewing/

Twitter@ three3sbrew

Tomfoolery in
Hammonton.

Tomfoolery Brewing

Located about thirty miles northwest of Atlantic City, the upward mobile town of Hammonton greets you with restaurants, charm, and friendly people, two of whom are husband-and-wife team, Shawn Grigus and Gayle D'Abate, owners of Hammonton's first craft brewery, **Tomfoolery Brewing**, a sprawling brewery located on Washington Street. Opened in December of 2015, **Tomfoolery** is a microbrewery whose aim is to bring great beer to South Jersey, as well as educate those who want to learn more about beer.

Shawn is no stranger to the beer world; he first started a homebrew shop called *Tap It* when he had difficulty finding ingredients and equipment for his hobby. He also started the very popular club, *Brew Jersey Home Brew Club,* a club dedicated to sharing the love of homebrewing. With brewing in his blood, it was a natural leap for Shawn to jump into starting a craft brewery. Though **Tomfoolery** is a production facility first and foremost, and located in an industrial space once used by the *Eastern Brewing Corporation*, a new tasting room offers 1,800 square feet of air-conditioned comfort. Look for the piano which guests are encouraged to play. If it's your lucky day, you might be treated to a song played by the young Colin, a delightful child and fledgling pianist.

Tomfoolery uses the best combination of science and engineering to craft excellent beer. Favorites include the ***Sun Grown IPA***, a hop forward beer with hints of citrus and white grape, and the ***Not So Old Bohemian***, an ode to Old Bohemian beer that used to be canned in the same facility. This pilsner is light and goes down easy*. **Crack Concrete***, a Belgian style tripel is another favorite.   **Tomfoolery** also offers seasonal beers, including an ***Oktoberfest*** in the fall.

While enjoying a flight or a pint, take a look at the old beer collection. The nostalgic feel of sipping *new* beer in a facility that used to can *old* favorites, can't be beat. Come try an ***Orbit the Sun*** Hefeweizen and a multitude of other great beers while having a tomfoolery of a great time at **Tomfoolery Brewing**. Leave the work to Shawn and Gayle. It's their pleasure.

Important Information:

Address: 334 N Washington Street, Hammonton, NJ, 08037

Phone: (609)561-1762

Website: www.tomfoolerybrewing.com

Email: contact@tomfoolerybrewing.com

Days and hours: Wed-Thurs 5-9, Fri 3-10, Sat 12-9, Sun 12-6

To go: growlers, beach growlers, 6 packs, kegs, specialty 22 oz bombers, cans (soon)

Events: Wed trivia, Tap it Thursday...try a new brew each Thursday, Fri $1.00 off full pours from 3-6pm, music (Check social media for schedule)

Social Media:

www.facebook.com/tomfoolerybrewing

www.instagram.com/tomfoolerybrew

Twitter@tomfoolerybrew

A Tuckahoe flight.

Tuckahoe Brewing Co.

Some of you craft beer newbies may have sat in the classroom with teachers Tim Hanna, Matt McDevitt, and Chris Konicki driving knowledge into your heads. If you were bad, you might have been sent to the principal's office, but if you were good, when you turned twenty-one, you might have been given a pass to their standout microbrewery. Actually, passes weren't given out, but they should have been, knowing that **Tuckahoe Brewing Co.** would brew such great beer that they'd outgrow their original location in Ocean View and four years later take on a larger space in Egg Harbor Township. The teachers, along with Jim McAfee and newer partner Stu Stromfield, have built a craft brewery more solid than a perfect four years on the principal's list.

After brewing in a garage and starting a small brewery in Ocean View, these partners worked themselves into what amounts to two full time jobs each, keeping their day jobs and spending hours keeping up with a demand that grew faster than their expectations. Two years ago, **Tuckahoe** left the Ocean View location and moved into its larger 10,000 square foot space which used to be occupied by a window and door company. Actually, the window and door company is still there, but has moved upstairs.

Tuckahoe Brewing Co. has sixteen beers on tap and a well rounded beer list with some traditional and many unique and innovative beers. Try their very popular *Quatrain*, an American IPA with notes of citrus, or their flagship *Dennis Creek Pale Ale*, an American pale ale with such a fragrant bouquet of floral and citrus, you might be instantly transported to an outdoor garden. Then, let your taste buds run wild with some imaginative special releases. Try a traditional *Berliner Weisse*, a cloudy sour beer served with your choice of a fruity syrup or coffee. How is that for something different?

Tuckahoe has a large and inviting tasting room with plenty of space to bring your coworkers for an awesome after work happy hour. And happy it will be. Come and enjoy. You'll be glad you listened to the teachers. They know what they're doing.

Important Information:

Address: 3092 English Creek Ave., Egg Harbor Township, NJ 08234

Guide to South Jersey Breweries

Phone: (609)645-2739

Website: www.tuckahoebrewing.com

Email: chrisktuckahoe@gmail.com

Days and hours: Thurs 4-9, Fri 3-9, Sat 12-8, Sun 1-6

To go: growlers, kegs, 6 pack bottles, 4 pack cans

Events: Thursday live music and food trucks, charity events (check social media)

Social media:

https://www.facebook.com/Tuckahoe-Brewing-Co-232894876731009/

https://instagram.com/tuckahoeco/

Twitter@TuckahoeCo

Jim, Tom, and Sue from Vinyl.

-Photo courtesy of Vinyl Brewing Co

*Vinyl Brewing Co (opening Fall 2017)

What do you get when you mix a beer brewing, punk rock drummer named Jim Sacco and husband-and-wife team, Tom and Susan Puentes, who always wanted to own a bar? Answer: A craft brewery that offers awesome beers and pays homage to the music scene. **Vinyl Brewing Co** is located at 300 12th Street in downtown Hammonton. This new craft brewery offers an excellent location, a fun spirit, and great beer.

Situated on the main drag and mere steps away from the center of town, Vinyl is surrounded by what makes Hammonton special: great food, a beautiful main street, and wonderful people.

The owners have taken an old door company,

gutted it, and modernized it into a welcoming space complete with a huge bar area and the unique feature of three glass garage doors that open up to the outside and let in the fresh air and charming ambiance of the town. An outdoor sidewalk seating area completes the inviting nature of this brewery. This three barrel brewery, where music and well made beer are central elements, is a welcome addition to the thriving town of Hammonton.

Vinyl Brewing offers rotating taps, which include IPAs, saisons, lagers, and sour ales. Barrel aged brews are the icing on the cake and will whip your palate into a frenzy for more.

Vinyl is the place to go for beer, a variety of music, and an ambiance that can't be beat. Do yourself a favor; go grab a friend and make **Vinyl Brewing** your next destination. You'll be glad you did.

Important Information:

Address: 300 12th Street, Hammonton, NJ 08037

Phone: (609)666-5460

Website: vinylbrewingnj.com

Email: vinylbrewingcompany@gmail.com

Days and hours: Tues-Thurs 3-9, Fri 3-10, Sat 12-10, Sun 12-8

To go: growlers, crowlers

Events: Check facebook page

www.facebook.com/vinylbrewing/

http://instagram.com/vinylbrewing

Twitter@vinylbrewing

There are two types of beer in the world: ale and lager.

Burlington County

Burlington County Beer Trail Map

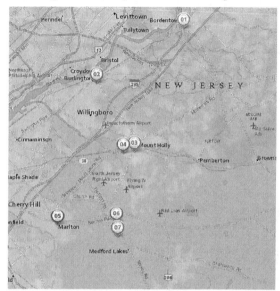

1)Common Sense 2) Third State 3)Spellbound 4) Village Idiot 5)Zed's Beer 6)Lower Forge 7)Nale House

Beer Trail One: Start at Common Sense in Bordentown. *Taste beer.* Drive twenty minutes via Rt 130 to Third State. *Taste beer.* From Third State drive twenty minutes to Spellbound via Mt. Holly Road. *Taste beer.* Then take the three minute drive down Washington Street to Village Idiot. *Taste beer.*

Beer Trail Two: Start at Zed's Beer. *Taste beer.* Drive ten minutes via Route 70 to Nale House. *Taste beer.* Walk a few blocks towards downtown and stop at Lower Forge. *Taste beer.*

Definition of a balanced diet?

A beer in each hand.

Beautiful downtown Bordentown, home of Common Sense Brewing.

Common Sense Brewing

Common Sense, a book written by Thomas Paine and published in 1776, challenged the authority of the British government and advocated for the independence of the colonies from Great Britain. One can't help but wonder if perhaps Great Britain wasn't importing good beer to the thirsty colonists.

Common Sense Brewing's name was influenced by Thomas Paine and his book, but there will be no need for independence here. Once you try the beer at **Common Sense**, you will, in fact, be giddily dependent. Some things you just won't want to give up.

Common Sense Brewing is located in the beautiful downtown distinct of Bordentown, only steps away from where Thomas Paine once owned a home. Set amongst the eclectic shops and wonderful restaurants on a brick lined street, you feel the sense of history around this craft brewery. In fact, America's first sculptress, Patience Wright, lived next door.

Started by longtime homebrewer Marc Selover, his wife, Robin, and Eric Eaves, **Common Sense** welcomes you with eight beers on tap. Their flagship *Paines Porter* is a hit. This chocolaty, dark beer, with hints of nuts, gets rave reviews. If you're not into dark beer, no worries, try the *Raspberry Saison*, a lighter, slightly sour beer. Or if you like IPAs, the *Crosswicks Creek IPA* will please you immensely. It's at once floral nosed and citrusy with hints of pine. Indecisive? Order a flight. This newer brewery will be serving up wheat beers as well. Make sure to check their website for the beer menu.

The expansive tasting room of brick and red is the perfect spot for a large gathering. Don't be shy about bringing the coworkers or a group of friends to enjoy a beer and then mosey over to one of the many wonderful restaurants in this town, growler in hand. Check *Downtown Bordentown's* website for a complete list of awesome events, too. **Common Sense** will be open for many of the festivals and functions this gorgeous town offers. Be sure to check their social media sites first.

As Thomas Paine once said, *"The world is my country, all mankind are my brethren, and craft beer is my religion."* * Well, honestly that is not quite the quote, but it should be after trying the *Paine's Porter*. Come to **Common Sense Brewing** today and indulge in one. You will leave a happy human.

Important Information:

Address: 102 Farnsworth Ave., Bordentown, NJ 08505

Phone: (609)526-8651

Website: https://www.commonsensebrewing.com

Email: info@commonsensebrewing.com

Days and hours: Fri 5-11, Sat 2-11, Sun 2-7

To go: growlers

Events: Check social media

Social media:

https://www.facebook.com/CommonSenseBrewing

https://www.instagram.com/commonsensebrewing

Twitter@CommonSenseBrew

*The original quote is attributed to Thomas Paine and reads, *"The world is my country, all mankind are my brethren, and to do good is my religion."*

Pola and Sean of
Lower Forge.

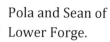

Lower Forge Brewery

Walking along the colonial style brick inlay through Main Street in Medford, you happen upon a beautiful, yellow stucco building surrounded by barrel style planters filled with colorful flowers. Once the home of the old Medford Print Shop, **Lower Forge Brewery** welcomes you first with its exterior, and then with its impressive interior. Romantic stringed lights adorn the ceiling and walls, lending to the relaxing feeling of being in an outdoor beer garden. Repurposed wood and windows add to its rustic, yet elegant décor.

Lower Forge Brewery is the perfect addition to this quaint town in Burlington County. Owned by the gracious and knowledgeable Sean Galie, his wife, Abbie, and his mother, Pola, **Lower Forge** has the feeling of family written all over it. In fact, this brewery is particularly family friendly, and even pet friendly. It's not unusual to see families enjoying food from one of the many surrounding eateries while chatting with Pola and friends. An outdoor seating area allows for enjoyment of a beautiful evening in the adorable town.

Brewing beer started as a stress relieving activity for Sean, who works as an EMT and firefighter. Soon mother and son were brewing batches of beer that impressed those who tried them. When asked about the size of the brewery, Sean states with a smile, "We are either the largest nanobrewery or smallest microbrewery in the state of NJ." Whatever they are, one thing is certain, the beer is excellent. Opened during American Craft Beer week in May 2016, **Lower Forge** is proud of brewing a variety of beers to please multiple palates, even those who are just entering the first craft beer stage...novice. After drinking years of Bud or Miller, delving into the world of craft beer can be both exciting and daunting. **Lower Forge** has a cure for that. One taste of their ***When Life Gives You Lemons*** radler and you will understand. It's delicious, crisp, and fresh; the perfect choice to please a rookie. Here, there is something to please every palate. Favorites include ***Legends and Lies*** Belgian ale, and the heartier, dry Irish stout, ***Major's Irish Stout***.

Lower Forge Brewery uses a pilot set up. The equipment is designed for experimental brewing, which allows the brewers to innovate more easily. As such, between seven and ten exciting beers are always on tap. Try the **_Watermelon Wanderlust_**, an innovative pale ale brewed with America's favorite melon.

Lower Forge is also exceptional in its care for the environment. Spent grain is brought to local farms to use as animal feed and fertilizer. Water used for cooling the wort is reclaimed and reused in the brewing process. **Lower Forge Brewery** is also energy efficient, works with local businesses for ingredients, and is supportive of local organizations.

Bring your appetite for great beer. This relaxed but lively, family owned brewery can't wait to meet you!

Important Information:

Address: 14 South Main Street, Medford, NJ 08055

Phone: (609)975-9532

Website: https://www.lowerforge.com

Email: brewery@lowerforge.com

Days and hours: Thurs 5-10, Fri 4-10, Sat 2-10, Sun 1-10

To go: growlers, six packs

Events: First Thursday open mic, Sunday book club, second and fourth Thursday trivia

Social Media:

https://www.facebook.com/lowerforge

https://www.instagram.com/lowerforgebrewery

Twitter@lowerforge

BREWERS ARE AT THE MERCY OF THE YEAST. THAT DARN YEAST WON'T TAKE A DAY OFF.

This beautiful cabinet was crafted by Dr. Rick Osler. It holds special meaning to Eric.

Nale House Brewing Co.

Upon first meeting **Nale House Brewing Co.** owner Eric Leiner, you notice his hair, and then you notice his heart. "I'm growing it to donate," he mentions, but only when asked. Eric and owners Anthony Zappy, Dave Harris, Sandy Harris, Tom Warner, and Dr. Mike Gollotto, have successfully turned a vacant hardware store into a hip and vibrant nanobrewery. Walking into the 2,500 square foot space, the unusual floor grabs your attention. "It was a mistake," Eric explains "but I liked how it looked, so I kept going." After ripping up carpet and sanding, what's left is a piece of modern art, a black floor with swirls reminiscent of fog. You might feel like you are walking in clouds on a stormy night.

Before opening **Nale House** in April 2016, Eric was already a presence in the quaint town of Medford. He owned a homebrew supply store in town. But surrounded by brewing equipment and ingredients, it seemed natural to take the next step into brewing craft beers and opening up a place where people could come and hang out. Each person to enter **Nale House** is treated as someone special. "We don't have customers;" Eric explains, "we have guests."

The forty nine seat brewery is unique in that it brews ales only; no lagers or sours. They specialize in barrel aged brews, and their ***Barrel Aged Farmhouse Saison*** is amazing. They will not reveal their brewing process, as it is top secret, but that is more than okay. Whatever they do, they do it well and produce high quality, brilliant beers.

Nale House believes in using local ingredients and joining forces with area restaurants. Medford's *Harvest Coffee Roastery's* coffee is used in their ***Coffee Stout***, and the restaurant *ITA 101* occasionally uses **Nale House** beer in some of their dishes.

When you visit **Nale House**, take a moment to admire the beautifully built, glass enclosed cabinet on the left wall. A special friend, Dr. Rick Osler, built the cabinet to house the unique beer can collection owned by Eric. The eclectic collection is displayed along with vintage nails, an ode to the old Nail House, now located on the Jennings Farm, where cut nail manufacturing was first introduced.

Stop by **Nale House Brewing Co.**, chat with the

gregarious Anthony, grab an excellent beer, and enjoy a seat at one of the beautiful, handmade tables of Japanese Sycamore or at the larger handmade Red and White Oak farmhouse style table. You're sure to meet a new friend.

Eric gives a big shout out to his parents, who have supported him in everything he's accomplished.

Important Information:

Address: 32 North Main Street, Medford, NJ 08055

Phone: (609)760-7246

Website: nalehousebrewing.com

Email: nalehousebrewing@gmail.com

Days and hours: Thurs 5-9, Fri 5-10, Sat 1-10

To go: growlers

Events: Music nights (check social media)

Social Media:

https://www.facebook.com/nalehousebc/

https://www.instagram.com/nalehousebc/

Twitter@NaleHouseBC

Long entryway
to Spellbound.

Spellbound Brewing

Let's be honest. Finding an entrance to a popular brewery by first locating the iron gate in the corner of a warehouse parking lot, which leads to a long corridor reminiscent of a street in a captivating European village, might not be easy. But lucky for you, now you know! Look for the iron gate in the corner of the parking lot. There will also be a sign. Then follow the yellow brick road to the entrance to **Spellbound Brewing**, though truth be known, the path is neither yellow nor brick, though the walls might be a close cousin!

Former homebrewers and now owners of Spellbound Brewing, Mike Oliver, Scott Reading, and John Companick are impressive young visionaries. **Spellbound** opened in October of 2014, as a booming production facility with a comfortable tasting room. Volume-wise, eighty percent of their beers go wholesale, but that doesn't stop the adoring public from pouring into the tasting room to sit at the long, wooden bar or to enjoy the outdoor space while sipping one of sixteen beers on tap, many of which are brewed exclusively for visitors.

The former *North Hampton Textile Warehouse* was originally supposed to be transformed into a production-only facility, but later when the laws changed, the tasting room was added before opening. **Spellbound** focuses on their brand, trying to keep the beers simple, consistent, and delicious. They shy away from calling their beers crazy names, except for their anniversary special beers with names such as, ***Living the dream?*** and ***What were we thinking?*** Humor is not lacking here, neither is kindness nor great beer.

Try the ***Major Nelson Pale Ale*** with hints of tropical citrus, or the simply named ***IPA***, both delicious and refreshing; and save room for the award winning ***Palo Santo Porter***, an outstanding porter that won a silver medal at the Great American Beer Festival.

Spellbound will continue to create awesome beer, especially with the new addition of a centrifuge in their brewing process, which allows them to spin the solids out of the beer, clarifying it before carbonation and packaging. This process leaves less suspended solids and contributes to a longer shelf life. Any spent grain is then sent to a local cattle farm.

A yearly **Spellbound** Century bike ride raises money for a chosen charity. This popular event fills up quickly, so if interested, check their social media sites early for information.

The only direction **Spellbound Brewing** is going is up. Come join the fun.

Important Information:

Address: 10 Lippincott Lane, Suite 12, Mt. Holly, NJ 08060

Phone: (609)832-0077

Website: www.spellboundbrewing.com

Email: info@spellboundbrewing.com

Wed 4-9, Thurs-Fri 4-10, Sat 12-8, Sun 12-5

To go: six packs, cases, growlers, kegs

Events: Spellbound Century, music (check social media)

Social Media:

https://www.facebook.com/spellboundbrew

http://instagram.com/Spellboundbrewing

Twitter@Spellboundbrew

John, Bill, and Jay enjoy their craft at Third State.

Third State Brewing

What do the first murder trial, second largest port in the new world, the oldest brew house in NJ, Ben Franklin, Ulysses Grant, and Isaac Collins have in common? They were located in or walked the streets of Burlington, NJ, a town whose vision for revitilization is accelerating by the day. This town with wide brick sidewalks is wonderful, with new businesses bolstering the downtown and interesting history everywhere. One such addition to the landscape of this charming town is **Third State Brewing**, located only two blocks from the Delaware River, and appropriately named for NJ being the third state to ratify the constitution.

Homebrewers Jay Mahoney, John O'Brien, and Bill Pozniak opened **Third State Brewing** in June of

2015. The three met at the homebrewing club called Barley Legal; please note the first part of the playful name is a *grain.* It takes a sense of humor to name all things beer related and also to brew it, especially if you scorch your second batch and have to throw it away. Good thing Jay, John, and Bill can chuckle at the trials and errors of 'raising' a brewery. We all benefit from their diligence and desire to brew great beer in this exciting microbrewery.

After searching for a location for a year and a half, the three found the perfect building in an old Farmers & Mechanics bank in Burlington, situated in the desirable downtown. The large space allows for a beautiful, high ceiling tasting room, as well as an impeccably clean back brewing area where **Third State** brews a spectrum of beers including lagers, IPAs, saisons, and stouts. Their flagship ***Boris the Younger Black Rye IPA***, a black beer with just enough rye to pleasantly sting your tongue, is really, really good. The ***Pour Visibility***, a New England IPA is another excellent choice. Made with Mosaic and Amarillo hops, it is sure to beg a second round. Whatever your taste, there is something for everyone. You can't go wrong with Bill as head brewer. He has over 20 years experience and is an award-winning homebrewer and recipient of a Pilsner Urquell award.

Do yourself a favor and get to **Third State Brewing**. The owners are fantastic and gregarious, the tasting room a comfortable space with really cool *see -through -to -the -hops* tables, and the beer is awesome.

Important Information:

Address: 352 High Street, Burlington, NJ 08016

Phone: (609) 387-1620

Website: www.thirdstatebrewing.com

Email: info@thirdstatebrewing.com

Days and hours: Thurs 5-9, Fri 5-10, Sat 2-11, Sun 2-7

To go: growlers, 22 oz bottles, kegs

Events: Live music/open mic a few times per month (check social media), Burlington Running Club meets on Thursday evenings

Social media:

https://www.facebook.com/Thirdstatebrewing

http://instagram/thirdstatebrewing

Twitter@3rdStateBrewing

Vince of Village
Idiot serves up a
pint.

Village Idiot Brewing Company

When you hear the words *village idiot*, a silly, fun-loving, nonsensical or worse, local resident might come to mind. But there is no "idiot" in this cozy, homey bar located right in downtown Mt. Holly, NJ, although you might earn that reputation should you NOT set foot through the door. The owner of **Village Idiot Brewing Company**, Vince Masciandaro, is the antithesis of a village idiot; in fact, he's an extremely intelligent civil engineer and crafty brewer.

Village Idiot opened in December of 2013, the first NJ craft brewery to open in a downtown location, trailblazing the way for other homebrewers to follow in their path. After homebrewing in college and some twenty five plus years afterward, Vince made the leap to open **Village Idiot** in what used to be the old Bridgetown Pub. The cozy interior immediately gives one a feeling of home; that chill and relaxed ahhhh. It's easy to see why friends would gather along the long, wooden bar or wooden pews and tables, or sit chatting in the lounge area with its comfortable leather couches and coffee table, although maybe more appropriately called a "beer table." It certainly feels like your neighborhood *Cheers.*

Vince used his civil engineering knowledge to build his own brewing equipment which he uses in the repurposed kitchen area of the old Bridgetown Pub. After tasting his beer, you might wish he would build some for you! The beer is incredible; no need for newfangled, fancy equipment here. Beers both traditional and what you might call "imaginative" fill the fourteen taps. Inventive flavors like ***Monkey Breath Banana Bread*** (ale poured into a sugar and cinnamon rimmed glass) and ***Philly Pretzel Ale*** are absolutely delicious. Or maybe you'd like to try the more traditional ***Hoptimizer IPA***, a customer favorite. Do as some of the locals do and mix a few. Try the ***Peanut Butter Cup*** mixed with the ***Monkey Breath Banana Bread*** for a flavorful combination you won't find anywhere else. Vince also brews seasonal favorites in the fall and winter. This craft brewery deserves its wins of the Best of Burlington County for the past four years! Stop on in. The beer at **Village Idiot Brewing Company** *"will make you awesome,"* and you'll definitely want to return for more!

Important Information:

Address: 42 High Street, Mt. Holly, NJ 08060

Phone: (609)975-9270

Website: villageidiotbrewing.com

Email: brewery@villageidiotbrewing.com

Days and Hours: Wed-Thurs 5-9, Fri 5-10, Sat 2-10, Sun 12-5
To go: growlers, crowlers

Events: Sunday open mic, Fire and Ice Festival, Acoustic Fridays, Trivia nights, much more (check facebook)

Social Media:

https://www.facebook.com/VillageIdiotBrewing/

https://www.instagram.com/villageidiotbrewing/

Twitter@VillageIdiotNJ

Enjoy a
flight at
Zed's.

Zed's Beer

You have to think that nothing but great beer could come from the great-grandson of a Hungarian miner who may just have inspired the "original growler"....well, kind of a growler. Great-Grandfather Zed, a coal miner and beer brewer, was known to brew such great beer that he wanted to share it with his neighbors in Hungary. According to family lore, he'd brew enough for a keg, hold a block party, and then start the flow of his magic liquid. Problem was, the keg was so heavy he couldn't stop the beer from coming out once tapped. So, he'd line up the neighbors, who held their pots and pans and whatever else they could get their hands on, and start filling until the keg was light enough to close the tap.

Years later, great-grandson Geoff Bado, together with his wife, Lori White, have honored Great-Grandfather Zed's memory by naming their craft brewery after him. **Zed's Beer** is now open in Marlton, NJ. Make sure you stop in; you'll see a portrait of the patriarch, Zed, overlooking the brewery, making sure the beer is brewed right...and boy is it!

Geoff started brewing over twenty years ago after receiving a Mr. Beer kit from Lori as a gag gift. After brewing what Geoff called a horrible first batch, he sought guidance from a homebrew shop and found that he started brewing better and better beer. He's been perfecting his craft ever since and decided to make the leap from five gallons to five barrels. When the town of Marlton approached Geoff about opening his craft brewery there, he accepted, and **Zed's Beer** was born.

This five barrel system brews up what Geoff calls "approachable craft." Most of the beers flowing from the twelve taps have an ABV of 5.5% and lower. At least four flagship beers will be standards and the rest, rotating taps. Try the flagship **Zed's in the Backyard—Copper Cream**, a delicious copper colored beer with a bit of a bite. **Zed's in Ireland— Dry Stout** is an excellent choice for stout drinkers. This dry stout has hints of both chocolate and coffee, and is really good. Though most of Zed's offerings are under ABV 5.5%, for those of you who enjoy a hearty IPA, Zed's offers **Zed's on the West Coast— IPA**, ABV 6%, a smooth IPA that's sure to please those who like a bit of hop in their step.

Zed's Beer is progressive in its sustainability and traceability. Spent grain is sent to a local farm in exchange for ingredients such as honey and peaches, both used in Zed's beers.

This family friendly craft brewery is ready to welcome you. Look for it on the far right of a strip mall on North Maple Ave in Marlton's historic district. **Zed's** aims to give you the true sensory experience of brewing. The tasting room, with tones of silver and cream, is open to the brewery, allowing one to see, smell, hear, and of course, taste the entire process. Stop in today, take a seat at the cool zinc bar handcrafted by Geoff and Lori, and bask in this craft beer adventure. The beer is sooo good.

Important Information:

Address: 19 N Maple Ave unit B, Marlton, NJ 08053
Phone: (856)872-7632
Website: http://www.drinkzeds.com/
Email: info@drinkzeds.com
Days and hours: Thurs 4-9:30, Fri 4-10, Sat 12-10, Sun 12-6
To go: growlers, crowlers soon
Events: See social media
Social media:
https://www.facebook.com/drinkzeds
https://www.instagram.com/drinkzeds/
Twitter: @drinkzeds

Camden County

Camden County Beer Trail Map

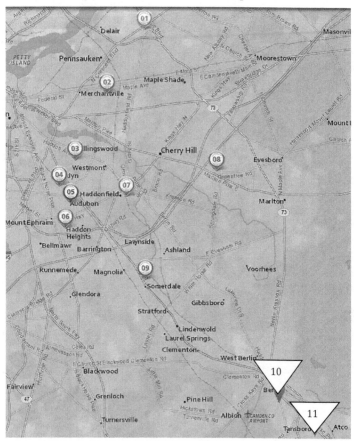

**11)Double Nickel 2)Eclipse 3)Devil's Creek
4)Tonewood 5)Red, White, and Brew 6)Lunacy
7)King's Road 8) Forgotten Boardwalk 9)Flying
Fish 10)Berlin 11) Atco**

Beer trail one: Start at Double Nickel. *Taste beer.* Drive seven minutes via Route 73 South and

then Park Ave to Eclipse. *Taste beer.* Drive ten minutes via Cuthbert Blvd and Haddon Ave to Devil's Creek. *Taste beer.*

Beer Trail two: Start at Tonewood. *Taste beer.*

Drive seven minutes via White Horse Pike to Red, White, and Brew (check that it opened). *Taste beer.* Drive four minutes via W Merchant Street and Hampshire Ave to *Lunacy.* (check that this location is open. If not, head to first location five minutes over at 214 Davis Rd, Magnolia). *Taste beer.* Head five minutes up King's Highway to King's Road (check that it's open). *Taste beer.*

Beer Trail Three: Start at Forgotten

Boardwalk. *Taste beer.* Drive fifteen minutes via 295 S and Burnt Mill Road to Flying Fish. *Taste Beer.* Drive fifteen minutes via S White Horse Pike to Berlin. *Taste beer.* Drive three minutes down S Horse Pike to Atco. *Taste beer.*

Please remember to have a designated driver or use a car service when following beer trails.

Many years ago, children drank beer because the water was unsafe. Women, the primary beer makers, brewed what they called

"little beer" for their children.

Serving up a pint at Atco

Atco Brewing Company

Nestled on a corner of a cozy strip mall on Route 30 in Atco, NJ, sits an unassuming nanobrewery with a large presence. Once inside **Atco Brewing Company**, it's understood why the owners picked the location. The space, complete with real German beer garden tables (biergarten for you fancy folks), is a comfortably large room of utilitarian décor, practical with the perfect touch of whimsy, as noted by the bright red pole that greets your eye upon arrival and the variety of games ready to be played by happy beer drinkers.

Twelve years ago, owners Shawn Iuliucci, Paul Lawyer, Dan Hoover, and Anthony Maccarella started brewing beer in a garage. Eventually, their hoppy hobby exceeded the square footage of that garage as demand from family and friends grew.

Hence, a brewery was born.

Using a unique three and a half BBL brewing system, one powered by steam to create a better boil, **Atco** creates such thirst quenching beers as stouts, IPAs, Trappist Ale, pilsners, *Blueberry Wheat* (a delicious wheat beer with a pleasant blueberry aroma and taste, thanks to local Hammonton blueberries), and favorites such as the double IPAs *Swellhead*, and *DIPcit*, the latter which gets its somewhat humorous name from a citra infusion.

Priding themselves on making simple, traditional beer with the highest quality ingredients, **Atco** is not a brewery to shy away from a good pilsner. A yearly Oktoberfest will feature their *Oktoberfest Pilsner*, one that is specially brewed and awaiting its October birth. **Atco Brewing Company** is well worth a visit. Come thirsty. The beer is great.

Important information:

Address: 302 White Horse Pike, Atco, NJ 08004

Phone: (856)292-9041

Web site: www.atcobrewing.com

Email: info@atcobrewing.com

Days and Hours: Thurs 5-9, Fri 3-10, Sat 12-10, Sun 12-5

To go: growlers, crowlers, cans

Events: Yearly Oktoberfest, check social media for other events

Social media:

www.facebook.com/atcobrewco/

http://instagram.com/atcobrewco

Twitter:@AtcoBrew

The baseball mural at Berlin Brewing Company.

Berlin Brewing Company

Remember when you were a kid and always wanted to hit that home run? Now is your chance at the home run headquarters of great beer, **Berlin Brewing Company**, a grand slam of a brewery. **Berlin Brewing Company**, owned by the athletic Joe Cruz and the beer maker extraordinaire, Tony Alfano, opened on November 21, 2015 in an old bus depot. Yes, the buses drove right through the building. Renovated to look like a baseball memorabilia collector's paradise (Joe's wife is happy it's out of the house), **Berlin Brewing Company** makes you feel like you slid into home plate at the bottom of the ninth to score the winning run. You smile when you walk in and just feel happy.

It's not just the décor; it's the beer too. Joe gives all the credit for the great beer to Tony, the head brewer. Tony, a nurse by trade, is as meticulous in his brewing process as he is in keeping the brew area spotless. What else would you expect from a nurse? Their flagship, **Boro Kolsch,** is a favorite, inspired by Tony's time spent in Germany. The beer menu, displayed as a starting lineup, also features the surprise hit tap filler **Humble Bitch,** as well as the **Insolent IPA**. The homemade root beer for those who have yet to acquire the fine palate of a seasoned beer drinker, is smooth and delicious.

Like challenges? Take the, "How many baseball mitts in the brewery?" challenge. In between sips of a **Nelson Hard Out Pale Ale** or **Blood Orange Shanty**, play detective to find all the baseball gloves. Who doesn't like a seek and find? While you are at it, ladies, take notice of the vintage victrola in the ladies' room, and men, of the vintage television set in the men's room. A special surprise will also greet the ladies once the door shuts. Promise, it is legal and sure to bring a giggle.

When you are finished, sit back down at the long bar made from tractor-trailer decking, listen to Joe tell some baseball stories from his time playing professional baseball, and make a new friend.

Important Information:

Address: 220 South White Horse Pike, Berlin, NJ 08009

Phone: (856)336-2038

Website: www. berlinbrewco.com

Email: berlinbrewco@gmail.com

Days and hours: Thurs-Fri 5-9, Sat 12-9, Sun 12-4

To go: growlers, crowlers, 3 packs

Events: Thursday live music (check social media), community charity events

Social media:

www.facebook.com/berlinbrewingcompany

www.instagram.com/berlinbrewing/

Twitter@BerlinBrewing

Anthony welcomes you to Devil's Creek.

Devil's Creek Brewery

Legend has it that years ago folks in the area of **Devil's Creek Brewery** spotted a funny flying, hooved creature with bat-like wings, horns, and the head of a goat, flapping its way over Newton Creek in Collingswood, NJ. The Jersey Devil, popular in NJ folklore, is said to have been spotted in the towns surrounding Newton Creek and Cooper River. Though a sighting can't be promised at the craft brewery, aptly named **Devil's Creek Brewery**, one thing is absolute; you *will* certainly spot more than a few tasty beers.

Devil's Creek Brewery opened on May 21, 2016 in the dry town of Collingswood, NJ. Owners Anthony and Kathy Abate took the happy gamble to open this main street location after Anthony had success in homebrewing and won several awards.

The wonderful vibe of this brewery is felt to the soul with its smiling, welcoming staff and happy patrons. Handcrafted chandeliers sculpted into works of art from reclaimed wood, join the handmade tables and a bar built from a roof rafter gathered from a razed 1870's era Philadelphia church. You might want to pray for guidance in selecting a beer at the bar, but there will be no need because the brewery is filled with kind patrons who will help you decide which beer to try and staff who are friendly and knowledgeable.

With twelve beers on tap and more than fifty brewed since the brewery's inception, you are sure to find something you love. Traditional flavors ranging from mild to bold are available, but be prepared to go crazy and try something imaginative and fun! Did you ever try *Birthday Cake* beer? You may have your chance to try that, or perhaps another inventive flavor dreamed up by Kathy.

Their flagship beer, *1888 Old Ale*, is popular and comes with a historical background. Collingswood used to be a town in which alcohol was served; however, it went dry in the year 1888. Being that **Devil's Creek Brewery** is the first establishment to manufacture and serve beer in Collingswood, it is apt that a beer is named for the year the town went dry. **Devil's Creek** brews its *1888 Old Ale* to closely mimic a beer from the year 1888, even using an ingredient called treacle, an uncrystallized syrup made during sugar refining, used in the earlier beer recipe. The result is delicious, refreshing, and moderately hoppy.

Other great choices include the ***Belma Pale Ale*** with its notes of citrus, or the barrel aged brew ***Nessie,*** a Scottish ale aged in a bourbon barrel for four months. Whatever you choose, you can't go wrong. All of the beers are poured with some level of nitrogen, creating a better mouthfeel and taste.

Apart from great beer, **Devil's Creek** is a green brewery. All cleansers used are both biodegradable and able to be metabolized. Can't get much greener than that!

Come now to **Devil's Creek Brewery** and have a devil of a good time; the beer is legendary, the location superb, and the camaraderie unparalleled.

Important Information:

Address: 1 Powell Lane (corner of Haddon Avenue), Collingswood, NJ 08108

Phone: (856)425-2520

Website: www.devilscreekbrewery.com

Email: info@devilscreekbrewery.com

Days and hours: Thurs-Fri 5-10, Sat 12-10, Sun 1-6

To go: growlers

Events: Trivia once a month, private parties

Social Media:

https://www.facebook.com/DevilsCreekBrewery

https://www.instagram.com/devils_creek_brewery/

Twitter@DevilsCreekBrewery

Beer dates back to around 9,500 BC. They must have been hoppy people.

Sweet Charlie at Double Nickel.

Double Nickel Brewing Company

Driving up to **Double Nickel Brewing Company,** after successfully navigating the jug handles and ramps of Pennsauken, you might feel like you came upon a beer museum enveloped in bright blue gift wrap. Truth is, **Double Nickel** is a gift, and that's made clear once you pull into the parking lot and spy the sign celebrating its first place lager at the 2017 AC Beer Fest. Museum it is not, but rather a large, inviting, industrial styled craft brewery; big enough for a party or two or three. If you are lucky, Charlie, the sweetest Golden Retriever this side of the Delaware, will greet you.

Owners Bob Dalsey, Bill Dalsey, Tom Dalsey, Mike Levy, Pete Liller, Mike Barret, Gary Woodand, Drew Perry, and Steve Yingling, have done a heck of a job taking an old Spa Fitness Gym, over 20,000 feet of it, and turning it into a facility with a huge tasting room, a mezzanine area big enough to host a party of one hundred, and a smaller back room fit for parties of thirty. Décor is sparse, but not needed, as your eyes are drawn to the sheer magnitude of the place, complete with exposed pipes and factory style ceilings. A bar with plenty of seating, outdoor space, and back room with a beanbag toss, confirm that this is place for fun and friendship.

But what's a great space without great beer? Here, your search for something to excite your beer taste buds will end. Owner Drew Perry has outdone himself in creating a variety of beers with something to please everyone. His years of experience brewing and creating recipes, has led to the success of **Double Nickel**. **Double Nickel Brewing Company** offers everything from IPAs to lagers; in fact, they offer three of the latter, and they take center stage. Best seller *Vienna Lager* is a good choice, offering a bite of malty goodness with a smooth finish. An impressive selection of Barrel aged beers (try the *Mother's Barrel* or the *Marbled Buffalo*) lends something extra special to this brewery, and a **DNA series** offers a new beer every other month.

Double Nickel Brewing Company uses NJ hops and honey and sends spent grain to area farmers, making it an excellent member of the community, one which cares about the environment and local farmers.

Be sure to stop in. Your toughest decision will be which beers to try.

Important Information:

Address: 1585 NJ-73, Pennsauken Township, NJ 08110

Phone: (856)356-2499

Website: http://dnbcbeer.com

Email: info@doublenickelbrewingcompany.com

Days and hours: Mon-Fri 4-10, Sat 12-10, Sun 12-5

To go: Growlers, crowlers, cans, bottles

Events: Every other Wednesday open mic, Quizzo, other (check social media)

Social media:

https://www.facebook.com/DoubleNickelBrewingCompany

http://instagram.com/doublenickelbrewingco

Twitter@dblnickelbrew

Pin where you are from at Eclipse.

Eclipse Brewing

It's a rare day when you walk to the backyard of an attractive business and see beautiful green Centennial hops climbing a trellis. But that's just what you'd expect after meeting a fun-loving man named Chris Mattern, owner of the "tiny" brewery, **Eclipse Brewing**. He's a man who enjoys the simple things in life, like horticulture and homebrewing. On Oct 8, 2016, Chris did something else he's always wanted to do, an idea sparked by his wife Beth; he opened a craft brewery in Merchantville, NJ. And though small, perhaps one of the smallest in the state, the beer at **Eclipse Brewing** is big on taste.

After looking for a suitable location, Merchantville emerged as a winner, a town that had lots of appeal but needed the foot traffic and pep of a craft brewery.

Indeed, the addition of **Eclipse** has forged relationships between the brewery and several restaurants through what Chris wittedly calls "cross-pollination." The quaint, house-style brewery is close to many restaurants of different cultures, including Japanese and Indian, as well as higher-end restaurants. Grab a growler before trying one, or get some takeout to bring into the tasting room. Everyone benefits, especially you.

Eclipse, though tiny, brews enough beer to fill seventeen taps. Try their hoppy flagship ***EPA IPA***, named after the street they are located on, East Park Ave. It's really delicious. If you like a bit of a bite, be sure to try the ***Peach Jalapeno Wit***, with just enough wow factor to taste the pepper without burning the tongue. **Eclipse** is the place to come if you have a friend who is new to the craft beer scene. They serve more soft noted fruity beers than most. And for the veteran drinker, you'll certainly have your choice of IPAs, stouts, wheats, and ales. It's amazing all that Chris can create.

The tasting room offers plenty of space to enjoy a conversation with a neighbor or a stranger, and some friendships have already been formed here. Chris tells the story of two neighbors who lived two doors away for years, but only met at the brewery. How is that for bringing people together? While enjoying the tasting room, make sure you look at the maps on the wall and place a pin where you are from. You'll be surprised to see that people from as far away as Ghana, Australia, and Canada have enjoyed beer at **Eclipse**.

Next time you are in Merchantville, be sure to stop at the little house on the corner next to the Merchantville biking/walking trail. There will be an **Eclipse Brewing** sign out front. There are plenty of parking spaces in the big lot next to and behind the brewery. Then head through the front door. You'll feel like you're coming home. You might never want to leave.

Important Information:

Address: 25 East Park Ave., Merchantville, NJ 08109

Phone: (856)662-7453

Email: eclipsebrewingnj@gmail.com

Days and hours: Wed-Thurs 4-9, Fri 4-10, Sat 12-10, Sun 12-8

To go: growlers

Events: Check facebook

Social Media:

https://www.facebook.com/Eclipse-Brewing

https://instagram..com/eclipsebrewing

The large tasting room at Flying Fish.

Flying Fish Brewing Company

Years after Marvin Gaye's songs were pressed into LPs and 45s in a Motown Records pressing plant, a businessman and brewery owner named Gene Muller was busy cleaning up the same 45,000 square foot warehouse to house his expanding business, **Flying Fish Brewing Company**. Unless you have just discovered the joys in drinking craft beer or have lived under a rock, you'd know the name **Flying Fish** is synonymous with awesome beer and sends fireworks though the soul. This craft brewery sits on five acres and is the first in South Jersey and largest in NJ. It is home to some of the most popular and interesting beers in the state.

Though it first opened in Cherry Hill in 1994, **Flying Fish** has been in its larger Somerdale location since 2012. Hard to miss with its bright yellow exterior and the edgy, but super cool **Flying Fish** logo out front, this massive facility still feels cozy and welcoming. The tasting room offers biergarten style tables which beg to invite company and new friends to sit, relax, and forget the world's problems. Though industrial in design, green plants and friendly faces from the well trained staff, make you feel at home.

But what about the beer? You must come and try it. **Flying Fish** abounds at area restaurants and package goods stores, but the fresh beer on tap in the tasting room will leave you salivating for more. The beers range from traditional to highly interesting. The ***Flying Fish Exit 13 Chocolate Stout*** is a sweeter, creamy stout with notes of coffee and chocolate. If dark beer is not for you, try the ***Flying Fish Extra Pale Ale***, with its medium hop nose and malt flavors. Or try something different like the ***Drunken Go-Nuts***, a cream ale style beer with hints of coffee. There's always something on tap on which to let your senses linger. Don't shy away from their barrel aged beauties. Your palate will thank you.

Whatever you try, you can bask in the knowledge that you are drinking a beer brewed by a company that cares about the environment. **Flying Fish Brewing Company** uses a state of the art brewing system which is highly efficient and allows for reuse, a gallon of water for every five gallons of beer brewed. They also have five hundred solar panels to help generate 10 % of the electric for the building and use LED lights and high efficient windows. If that isn't enough, seven hundred fifty tons of spent grain was sent to dairy farms in the last year alone.

   Stop on over and try a few beers. Then head over to Philly to check out their **Flying Fish Craft House**, a brewpub featuring their numerous beers. In either location, you will leave happily floating on air, much like their cherished flying fish logo.

Important Information:

Address: 900 Kennedy Blvd, Somerdale, NJ 08083

Phone: (856)504-3442

Website: www.flyingfish.com

Email: info@flyingfish.com

Days and Hours: Wed-Fri 3-9, Sat 12-6, Sun 12-6

To go: growlers, kegs, bottles, other

Other: retail store off tasting room

Events: Bike race, Fun ride, 5K, Somerdale Day biergarten, community events (Check social media sites for event dates)

Social media:

www.facebook.com/flyingfishbrew

www.instagram.com/flyingfishbrew/

Twitter@flyingfishbrew

Skee-ball fun at Forgotten Board

Forgotten Boardwalk

No time to hit the beach this year, but miss the nostalgic feel of the shore's aquamarine splendor? No problem; a fun, microbrewery, with charming boardwalk touches, will make you feel like a kid walking down memory lane, though with a beer in hand rather than sticky cotton candy of days past. Owner Jamie Queli, a homebrewer for more than ten years, has taken her ample business experience and combined it with her love of brewing and NJ, to create one of the most creative breweries you will ever set foot in.

Forgotten Boardwalk Brewing Co., located in the space previously occupied by *Flying Fish*, can be a bit challenging to find. Be sure to enter the parking lot at 1940 Olney Ave and head to the far left of the building. There you will be welcomed with aqua colored beach chairs and the feeling that the enjoyment is about to begin, as evidenced by the almost human sized connect four game. Upon walking through the door, your senses soar and you might feel like time has regressed. Color abounds in this brewery, with skee-ball and boardwalk games sprinkled throughout. Do you remember the crazy mirrors of the fun house? This place has them. We wouldn't recommend drinking too much before standing in front of one; you might let out a squeal. But we do recommend drinking the beer!

Forgotten Boardwalk has a fun portfolio of beer. Though they consider themselves mild traditionalists and tweak some styles, they don't like to follow trends, but rather let the beer speak for itself. Besides the obviously fun games, their flagship beer ***Funnel Cake***, lends to the theme and an amusing experience. This Boardwalk cream ale has aromas of vanilla, a creamy mouthfeel, and a smooth, sweet finish. You might be reminded of a funnel cake dipped in cream soda. It's both interesting and really delicious.

If funnel cake is not your thing, try the ***1916 Shore Shiver***, an IPA with a bite, brewed to pay homage to the 1916 shark attacks which occurred off the NJ shore. In fact, each July, look for the *Shark Attack IPA* event. You will enjoy shark themed beers, games, and more. But no matter what beer you try, be sure to notice the names. **Forgotten Boardwalk** heavily brands with names related to the history of NJ.

So come, take a trip down memory lane, tantalize your palate, and have a great time. Only the logoed boardwalk cats will know what happens here. And we promise they won't tell.

Important Information:

Address: 1940 Olney Ave #100, Cherry Hill, NJ 08071

Phone: (856)437-0709

Website: www.forgottenboardwalk.com

Email: info@forgottenboardwalk.com

Days and hours: Mon 12-6, Thurs 4-8, Fri 4-9, Sat 12-9, Sun 12-8

To go: growlers, cans, special bottle releases, kegs

Events: Cat adoption once a month, Annual Spice of Life Organ Donation event, The Shark Attack IPA event each July, more (check website)

Social media:

https://www.facebook.com/ForgottenBoardwalk

https://www.instagram.com/forgottenboardwalk

http://www.pinterest.com/forgottenboards

Twitter@ForgottenBoards

Beautiful Haddonfield!

*King's Road Brewing Company (opening fall 2017)

When King Charles II ordered his henchmen to build the 1,300 mile road connecting Charleston, SC and Boston, Mass, he had no idea that a group of ambitious, caring individuals in NJ would give recognition to that road by naming their nanobrewery after it. Located on Kings Highway, **King's Road Brewing Company** is the brainchild of Jeff Farrell, Pete Gagliardi, Bob Hochgertel, Chris Thomas, and Victoria Cummins. Together this group of individuals is a superpower; each deeply involved in their town of Haddonfield and committed to bettering their community.

Adding a brewery to the historically dry town was a natural step for them. After seeing other towns flourish with activity with the addition of a craft brewery, the group wanted to fertilize their own community and help it thrive. Haddonfield, boasting so much charm already that it's about to burst, was a natural fit.

King's Road Brewing Company is located, coincidentally, in the old Gibbs' Tavern and Smithy, a building dating back to 1777. What better place to house a friendly, downtown craft brewery? Perhaps it was a sign or synchronicity, but it seems that Mr. Gibbs was missing his beer. This spanking new brewery serves up such favorites as ales, saisons, sessions, IPAs, wheat beers, and more.

King's Road utilizes a unique brewing system that uses two floors due to the building constraints. On the second floor, the first process of the beer making takes place. After fermenting, gravity takes over and sends the beer into the brite tanks to finish and carbonate in the basement, where the cold room is also located. It's only a short trip from the cold room to your glass and a thirst quenching experience from one of four to six regular beers and six rotating beers on tap, each with a name paying homage to the history of Haddonfield and the surrounding area.

Come hungry! Haddonfield doesn't only have great craft beer, but also great restaurants. You'll love this town so much you'll want to return, and the ambiance and historical nature of **King's Road** will have you dreaming of the next time you'll drive up a portion of King's Highway to the town's newest craft brewery.

Important information:

Address: 127 Kings Highway East, Haddonfield, NJ 08033

Phone: (855)577-3196

Email: info@kingsroadbrewing.com

Days and Hours: Tue, Wed, Thurs 5-10, Fri 4-10, Sat 12-10

Website: kingsroadbrewing.com

Events: Yes, check social media for updates

Social media:

www.facebook.com/KingsRoadBrewing/

http://instagram.com/kingsroadbrewing

Twitter@KingsRoadBrew

Kick up a good
time at Lunacy.

Lunacy Brewing Company

When Michael Lees, Ricky Lees, Jay Macrina, and Ed Gledhill opened the doors of **Lunacy Brewing Company** in January of 2015, they never imagined it would grow in size fifteen-fold within just a few years. Transitioning from a one barrel 990 square foot space to a fifteen barrel 4,000 foot space in less than three years, says a lot about the kind of beer and atmosphere this brewery serves up. The original, smaller space is slightly hard to find, as the entrance is around the back of an old warehouse; but once found, industrial charm abounds and the vibe is felt through all its guests, even the little ones. Imagine a brewery complete with slides and games for the kids in a fenced-in backyard. You get the picture.

Friendly, comfortable, relaxed, and tremendously non-stuffy, this brewery boasts a speakeasy feel, filled with laughter and happy faces.

The new location on Kings Highway in Haddon Heights is like a bigger twin sister. The owners really wanted to bring the original vibe to the newer space, and they have succeeded. The 1,000 foot tasting room has the same décor and feel as its little sister. The entrance, again, is around the back, so don't be shy in looking back there. A large grassy area will once more allow for play and fun for all patrons, and a garage door will open from the inside to allow for that outdoor feeling while sipping great beer.

Lunacy has a full menu of beers on tap from IPAs to porters, stouts, saisons and barrel aged. Try the popular *Lunacy IPA*, a well balanced East Coast style IPA with just the right amount of hoppiness and bitterness to make your kisser grin. Their *C-3PA* IPA is another great choice with a citrus tango waiting to dance in your mouth. Like something different? Try the *Rocket Chocolate Peanut Butter Stout*; it might remind you of a favorite candy bar with an adult, liquid twist.

Whatever you drink, there are a few things you should notice while there. First, admire the awesome flight boards handcrafted by the talented Jason Whitcraft. Each board is a work of art and a great conversation piece. Not sure what to say to your date? These boards will give you a start. Also, check out the vibrant and totally wondrous grandfather clock decorated with hundreds of beer caps. It's fun and unique.

   Do yourself a favor and go to **Lunacy Brewing Company**. You will be welcomed, encouraged to let your hair down, and made to feel at home.

Important Information:

Address: 1500 West Kings Highway, Haddon Heights, NJ 08035

Phone: (856)282-6300

Website: http://lunacybrewingcompany.com/

Email: info@lunacybrewingcompany.com

Days and Hours: Thurs 5-9, Fri 5-10, Sat 1-8, Sun 12-5 (Check website to see if hours change upon move to this location.)

To go: growlers and crowlers soon

Events: Vinyl Saturdays. Bring your own records, if desired (BYOR)

Social Media:

www.facebook.com/LunacyBrewing/

www.instagram.com/lunacybrewingcompany/

Twitter@ lunacybrewing

What is red, white, and brew all over?

Easy! A red checkered tablecloth covered in spilled beer.

Oh, and a great new brewery!

*Red, White, and Brew Beer Company (spring 2018)

This craft brewery which takes their name to honor the American craft beer scene and its blazing path of innovation, aims to open in early spring of 2018. They believe in the importance of keeping small business and community alive. Their new downtown location will be a welcome addition to Audubon and will be serving up great beer. This community driven group of craft beer lovers aims to serve classic style beer in a place where everyone will feel welcome. We can't wait until they are open!

Important Information:

Address: 100 W Merchant St, Audubon, NJ 08106

Website: www.redwhiteandbrewbeercompany.com

Days and hours: Check website

To go: Will have growlers and sixtels

Social media:

https://www.facebook.com/Red-White-and-Brew-828029287325627/

https://www.instagram.com/redwhiteandbrewbeerco/

Twitter@RedWhiteBrewBC

Tonewood's beautiful tasting room.

Tonewood Brewing

Germany is home to some really great beer styles, and Eli Facchinei is no stranger to that. In fact, after traveling to Germany, he was so enamored with German beer culture that he knew when he returned, he wanted to brew his own beer. After learning the ropes and working as a brewer in Colorado, he decided to make his passion his own, to start and own a brewery where great beers are brewed. Eli enlisted the help of brother, Taylor, and dad, Jim, and got busy. **Tonewood Brewing,** its name born of the family's interest in music and the tonal quality of string instrument wood, was conceived.

It wasn't so easy. First, finding a location without red tape was a challenge. Enter Robert Forbes, mayor of Oaklyn who heard that the guys were looking for a suitable downtown location. When the mayor reached out, things began to happen, and Oaklyn is reaping the benefits of that helping hand. **Tonewood** has built a reputation for having some of the finest beers around; in fact, in its first year they have doubled their capacity and built a steady customer base.

Tonewood offers an absolutely beautiful tasting room, so warm and inviting. Imagine a downtown location, walkable and accessible, with a plenty of street parking and a large side parking lot. It gets better. Now imagine walking into a well decorated space with the cozy touches of brick on the wall, wood ceilings, a fantastic ash bar, and handcrafted tables made from local milled wood. Add in a couple of garage doors that open to an outdoor biergarten and you've entered the environment of dreams. That is **Tonewood's** reality.

But as we know, a beautiful tasting room is nothing without great beer. **Tonewood Brewing** delivers this too. **Tonewood** brews what they like to call classic styles with modern interpretations. They brew everything from IPAs to lagers to pilsners to saisons and more. Their popular *Fuego IPA* is cloudy and hop forward with just the right amount of bitter to make one seek another sip. *Stella Blue* is another triumph. This easy drinking pale ale with blueberries has just enough blueberry 'tart' to remind you of Grandma's pie. Blueberries are not your thing? Try **_Poolside Lager_**, a 5.2% ABV Mexican lager brewed with traditional lager yeast. It's so refreshing you will feel like your toes are dipped in cool water. Whatever you try, you will not be disappointed. Attention to quality and taste is apparent.

Looking for something different to do? Check out their Bluegrass jam on the second Wednesday of each month. You will want to tap your shoes in time with the music as you sip an awesome beer. Come give **Tonewood Brewing** a try. You will feel amazing.

Important Information:

Address: 215 West Clinton Ave, Oaklyn, NJ 08107

Phone: (856)833-1500

Website: www.tonewoodbrewing.com

Email: tonewoodbrewing@gmail.com

Days and hours: Tue-Fri 4-10, Sat 12-10, Sun 12-7

To go: 6 packs, growlers, crowlers

Events: every second Wednesday Bluegrass Jam, Final Friday Food trucks (fourth Fridays)

Social Media:

http://www.facebook.com/tonewoodbrewing

https://instagram.com/tonewoodbrewing

Twitter@TonewoodBrewing

Cape May County

Cape May Beer Trail Map

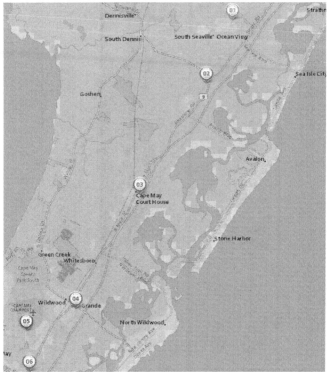

1)Ludlam Island   2)Slack Tide   3)Bucket Brigade
4)7Mile 5)Cape May 7)Cold Springs

Beer Trail Map One: Start at Ludlam Island.

Taste beer. Drive seven minutes via Corson's Tavern
Road and Kings Highway to Slack Tide. *Taste Beer.*
Drive ten minutes south on Route 9 to Bucket
Brigade (check that they have opened). *Taste beer.*
Drive eleven minutes via Garden State Parkway to 7
Mile. *Taste Beer.*

Beer Trail Two: Start at Cape May. *Taste Beer.*
Drive seven minutes via Breakwater Road and
Seashore Road to Cold Springs Village. Brewery on
left of parking lot. *Taste beer.*

Some of 7 Mile's offerings.

7 Mile Brewery

When IT executive and Pit Master turned brewer, Pete Beyda, and his close friend and realtor, Chris Collett, turned a Cape May County retail store front into a thriving brewery, they not only set out to brew great beer but also to impact the community in a positive way. **7 Mile Brewery**, in Rio Grande, lives up to its motto: *Making great beer, Serving great people, and Building a great community.* This craft brewery just celebrated their first anniversary on Sept 2, 2016, but they have already raised over $10,000 for local charities. **7 Mile** really emphasizes the importance of community and caring for people. What better place to drink a beer than in a brewery which holds humanity in high regard.

7 Mile has an expansive tasting room tastefully decorated in shades of dark blue and silver. There is

127

plenty of seating available at the long, tall beer tables. Here you can relish one of the twelve to fourteen beers **7 Mile** has to offer. With six flagships and many rotating and seasonal beers, there is something for everyone.

   7 Mile Brewery doesn't just build hoppy beers; they think of beer brewing as a fine craft, and brew a variety of beers, all with character. Settle down with a **7 Mile IPA**, a session with fruit and citrus notes; a great choice after a hot beach day. Perhaps you're in the mood for a richer beer, something dark, chocolaty, with notes of coffee and the added zing of nitro. That's their **Shorty Stout on Nitro**.   Want something different? Try many of their interesting specialty or seasonal beers, such as an English Porter like **Bosco's Revenge**, a smoked beer flavored with bacon from a local butcher and malts smoked in the smoker. Remember, Pete *is* a Pit Master. Seasonals include a Belgian Wittier called **Beach Bubbles**, **Rue 9**, a peach saison, and **Red, White, and Bru**, a saison with tart cherry.

   One thing is certain; you will meet a new friend. The fifty foot bar and many tables beg for friendly conversation amongst beer loving patrons. Vacationers and locals will clank glasses trading stories and pleasantries. On nice days, an outdoor biergarten adds to the fun with yard games available to be played under Cape May sunshine. Stop by today. **7 Mile** beers are waiting to hug your palate.

Guide to South Jersey Breweries

Important Information:

Address: 3156 Route 9 South, Rio Grande, NJ 08242

Phone: (609)365-7777

Website: www.7milebrew.com

Email: info@7milebrew.com

Days and hours: Mon-Sat 12-10, Sun 12-6

To go: growlers, cans

Events: Tuesday quizzo 7-10, Sat and Sun music in summer, check schedule for fall music events

Other: Look for expansion of 7 Mile into Philadelphia!

Social media:

https://www.facebook.com/7milebrew

https://www.instagram.com/7milebrew

Twitter@7milebrew

-Graphics courtesy of 7 Mile Brewery

The guys at Bucket Brigade are ready to
welcome you!

*Bucket Brigade Brewery (Opening fall 2017)

Let's face it; we all get hot, whether from the sharp rays on a sunny day, a red-faced argument, a glance from a nice looking person, or from the rage of a roaring fire. Wouldn't it be great to douse that fire and quench that thirst with an excellent beer brewed by firemen? Who better would know what it takes to cool down a parched mouth? Welcome to **Bucket Brigade Brewery**, an exceptional brewery built by two homebrewing, fire-fighting brothers, Karl and Kurt Hughes, and their longtime, beer brewing friend, Mark McPherson Jr. With homebrewing a part of their lives and public service a part of their blood, the brothers wanted to combine their passions and create a brewery where community and beer exist together with honor. The founders felt a sense of duty as strong as their service, to build a place where the beer is worthy of the citizens they serve.

The tasting room brings in another passion: history. The very building in which **Bucket Brigade** operates is part of the brothers' family narrative. The building that used to be H.B. Christman and Sons was owned by their uncle from 1949-2006. Though it was later sold, it is now embracing the dreams of his nephews. It also sits well with the theme, and with a firehouse look, it is the perfect fit.

While visiting the tasting room, look for images and relics from various businesses that had once operated in Cape May County. And while admiring the historical décor, be sure to indulge in a pilsner, ale, or lager, all brewed in small batches to ensure that the beer is consistent and top notch.

Be sure to check out **Bucket Brigade's** social media sites for event information. This new brewery is ready to please your palate and serve up a good time.

Important Information:

Address: 205 N Main St., Cape May Court House, NJ

Phone: (609)778-2641

Days and Hours: Please check website or social media for updates

Web: www.bucketbrigadebrewery.com

Social media:

www.facebook.com/bucketbrigadebrewery

www.instagram.com/bucketbrigadebrewery

Twitter@BucketBrew

Events: Yes, check website or social media for updates.

-Graphic and photo courtesy of Bucket Brigade

The expansive tasting room at Cape May Brewing Co.

Cape May Brewing Company

Even the most celebrated microbrewery in Cape May can learn a good lesson. The first batch of beer ever brewed at **Cape May Brewing Company** by owners Ryan Krill, Bob Krill, and Chris Henke, resulted in a nightmarish mess because of the 'drain to nowhere.' Two hundred gallons of water actually drained into a wall rather than the working drain they assumed it was. After spending their entire first night cleaning up the flood, the gritty group kept ticking, building a fun, crowd pleasing, and lively craft brewery located at the Cape May Airport.

This brewery, housed in a bright blue, warehouse-style building, first takes its visitors on a tour through its brewing area, offering an interactive style experience reminiscent of a please touch museum. Soon after, the tour weaves its way into the expansive tasting room. Though sometimes bursting with visitors, there is a method to their hoppy madness, and the lines move quickly.

And why wouldn't this place be popular? Opened in 2011, **Cape May Brewing Company** has a beer for every taste. With twenty brews on tap, from traditional to those tumbling with originality, their variety can't be beat. The flagship *Cape May IPA* is the right combination of bitter and hoppy, a delicious brew that has made many a mouth smile. Other great choices include the Double IPA, *Coastal Evacuation*, a West Coast style DIPA with Centennial hops offering hints of orange and honeydew, and the Belgian strong *Devil's Reach*, a complex, yet fruity and light beer. The *Honey Porter*, a Silver Award winner in the porter/stout category of the National Honey Board, is one of only two Jersey Fresh certified beers in the state.

Cape May is constantly trying to push the envelope when it comes to creating new and interesting beers. Their barrel-aged series includes the extraordinary *Top Sail* which was rated 98 by Beer Connoisseur. **Cape May Brewing Company** also has a dedicated sour brewery, the only one in the state. Look for it on the tour, then let your mouth pucker in shameless guilt with a taste.

Going with a group? No problem. There are enough

long biergarten-style picnic tables to seat an army and some outdoor games to keep the fun flowing under the outdoor tent. And for the non-beer drinker, there are some delicious sodas to wet your fancy. Come one, come all, and see what the fuss is about. You will soon have another reason besides the sun and sand to head to Cape May, and **Cape May Brewing Company** might soon become your *only* reason.

Important information:

Address: 1288 Hornet Rd., Cape May, NJ 08204

Phone: (609) 849-9933

Website: capemaybrewery.com

Email: beer@capemaybrewery.com

Days and Hours: Open 7 days a week 11am-9 pm

Offseason hours are 12pm-8pm

Closed Christmas, Easter, Thanksgiving

To go: growlers, bottles, cans

Other: The Brewtique gift shop

Events: One-Off Wednesday kegs, special soda Thursdays, beer sponsor for the Cape May Exit Zero Jazz Festival, team sponsor for the BikeMS: City to Shore Race, Fourth of July weekend anniversary party, Ugly Sweater Contest at Christmas, numerous special events-check website.

Social Media:

https://www.facebook.com/CapeMayBrewCo/
https://twitter.com/capemaybrewco
https://www.instagram.com/capemaybrewco/
https://vimeo.com/capemaybrewco
https://untappd.com/CapeMayBrewingCompany

Cleanliness in brewing is everything.

The beautiful backyard at Cold Springs Brewery.

Cold Spring Brewery

Way back in 1804, a few miles north of the historic Cold Spring Village, stood a barn used to store grain and animal feed. Flash forward to July 2016, and again the barn stands, as the rustic and fun **Cold Spring Brewery**, reconstructed board by board in its newest location of Cold Spring Village.

The first thing you feel when you pull into the white gravel parking lot of the village is an immense pull to enter the quaint barn to the left of the lot. You sense the rural feel of living on a farm, excitement of exploring a historic relic, and the outdoorsy feel of camping, all rolled into one. You just want to go in and see what is there. Will there be animals? Old tools? Hidden treasures?

141

We can't promise you animals, though pets are welcome, but we can promise the unexpected...great beer. And yes, you will also see such goodies on the walls as old farming yokes, vintage saws, mallets, and wooden vises. It's just the sort of atmosphere you'd want to enjoy should you feel the need to quench the beer bug and take in a bit of American farming history.

When finished admiring the interior, grab your beer and stroll around the back and relax by the fire pit or play yard games with the family.

Though keeping with the history of brewing beer, **Cold Spring Brewery** creates a menu of beers fit for modern day times. Their most popular beer, ***Cold Spring Red***, has a slight malty flavor and is delicious. Other popular choices include the ***Cresse American Wheat***, a hazy gold beer with a citrus and grain aroma. It is light and crisp. The ***Hildreth German Wheat***, a hefeweizen with a nose of banana and cloves, satisfies and pleases the palate.

When you are finished tasting the beer, do yourself a favor and stroll through the Cold Spring Village itself. This open air, living history museum, educates its guests with a walk through early American history. Enjoy the feel of an early American town alone or with others. The village is meant to be enjoyed with family and the brewery is family-friendly, so do bring the kids.

The Foundation of Cold Spring is a nonprofit that oversees both the village and the brewery. The three barrel nanobrewery helps fund the village. Your purchase of a beer at **Cold Spring Brewery** will help keep history alive in this cultural museum... for many years to come.

Important Information:

Address: 733 Seashore Road, Cape May, NJ 08204

Phone: (609)854-3077

Website: https://coldspringbrewery.org

Email: 4info@hcsv.org

Days and Hours: Tues-Sun 12-8 (7 days in July and August)

Events: Thankful Thursday every Thursday where they donate a percentage of profits to nonprofits, many events in conjunction with the village (check social media)

Social Media:

https://www.facebook.com/TheColdSpringBrewery

https://www.instagram.com/coldspringbrewery

Can you imagine this in your mouth? Ludlam
Island is ready to serve you.

Ludlum Island Brewery

Located only ten minutes inland from Sea Isle, in a very quiet and green area of Ocean View, NJ is a small craft brewery that carries a big punch. Though the warehouse-style building in which **Ludlam Island Brewery** resides is large, the tasting room is comfortably small, but big enough to have plenty of room in which to mill around or sit and unwind.

Ludlam Island Brewery is named for Ludlum Island, the island in which Sea Isla and Strathmere are located. The brewery is not actually on the island, but slightly off the beaten path and very easy to find. The location is really lovely. Surrounded by green and peace, you get that quiet feeling needed when you've spent too much time sandwiched between hordes of beach goers and shore craziness. Go, you must. This brewery offers eight beers on tap, from

IPAs to ales to stouts and more. They even brew delightful cask beers, smaller, less carbonated batches of beer with added flavor and served a bit warmer. So good.

Ludlam Island Brewery was opened in June of 2016 by homebrewers who have been brewing up flavorful beers since college. Knowing their beer was good enough to make a mark; they took the leap and opened the craft brewery. Try their flagship *Fish Alley IPA* or *Harry's Coffee Pale Ale*, a rye pale ale flavored with *Harry and Beans* coffee beans. Another popular favorite is *Lamplight IPA*, a hop forward... and forward...and forward beer. Yes, it's hoppy but awesome. It's a hazy IPA with notes of tropical fruit.

This super clean craft brewery is awaiting your arrival. Stop on in and try a well crafted beer while admiring the cozy décor complete with reclaimed wood. You'll feel like you're at the most relaxing place near the shore, minus the sand between your toes.

Important Information:

Address: 9 Stoney Ct, Unit 3, Ocean View, NJ 08230

Phone: (609)263-6969

Website: www.ludlamisland.com

Days and hours: 7 Days a week 12-8

To go: growlers, crowlers, cans in near future

Guide to South Jersey Breweries

Events: yoga, special event parties (check social media)

Social media:

https://www.facebook.com/ludlamisland

https://www.instagram.com/ludlamisland

Twitter@LudlamIsland

https://untappd.com/LudlamIslandBrewery

The people at Slack Tide are as
awesome as the beer!

Slack Tide Brewing Company

When an ocean tide energetically licks the beach hard, we all know that we need equal energy to hold onto our swimsuits. But there is something magical in a tide, the peace that comes right between the ebb and flow of the water, calm called slack tide... serenity... and the perfect break for a beer. Enter the energetic ebb and flow of two brothers named Jason and Tadhg Campbell, homebrewers and avid fishermen who crafted such great beer that their friends and family urged them to open a brewery. Lucky for everyone, they listened, and brought to the world a place where you can feel at peace and unstressed, a place to relax and unwind with a great beer, **Slack Tide Brewing Company**.

To find **Slack Tide**, keep an eye on out for the *Cool Tronics* sign with **Slack Tide** listed just below; the brewery is on the left back side of the creamy yellow, warehouse style building. Once inside, your own emotional slack tide will appear and calm will unfold. But don't let that stop you from having a good time. Here, laughter and fun abounds and the bartenders are always smiling. The ambiance is welcoming and reminiscent of a home at the seashore: pale blues and bleached, reclaimed wood adorn the ceiling, bar, and walls. The tasting room is comfortably cozy, but if you head to the back room where the beer is brewed, there is even more seating. Two times the ambiance... nice.

Atmosphere in a brewery is always a plus, but great beer is a bigger plus. **Slack Tide Brewing Company** does not disappoint. With their addition of a new ten barrel system, not only will they continue serving awesome beer, but more innovative beers too. Try their ***Flagship Angry Osprey***, a 6.8% ABV IPA, hop forward with notes of pine and citrus. ***Angry Osprey*** took fifth in the Brewvitational in 2016. Or try the award winning favorite, the ***Bell Bouy***, a slightly sweet Belgian blonde with enough of a white head that you might leave with a little mustache.

Knockdown is another must try. This black IPA took third at the Best of Craft Beer awards. Because the beer is so good, you might decide on a flight and add a **Monkey Face American Stout** or the **Stone Harbor Wheat**.

Whatever you do, you will feel both relaxed like a slack tide when leaving and somehow energized from the experience. Don't miss this craft brewery. **Slack Tide** is waiting to welcome you.

Important Information:

Address: 1072 Rt 83, Unit 3, Clermont, NJ 08210

Phone: (609)478-2343

Website: www.slacktidebrewingco.com

Email: slacktidebrewing@gmail.com

Days and hours: Mon, Wed, Thurs 2-8, Fri- Sun 12-8

To go: Growlers, crowlers

Events: See social media

Social media:

http://www.facebook.com/slacktidebeer

http://instagram.com/slacktidebeer

Twitter@SlackTideBeer

Beer cans were introduced in 1933.

"Can you drink this beer?" he asked.

"I think I can. I think I can."

Cumberland County

Cumberland County Beer Trail Map

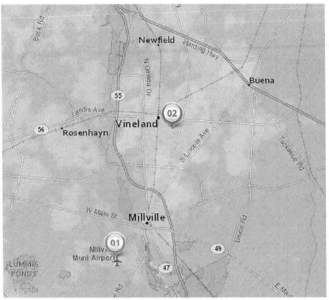

1) Glasstown 2) Brinx Jones

Beer Trail One: Start at Glasstown. *Taste beer.*
Drive twenty two min via Route 555 to Brinx Jones
(check that it has opened*). Taste beer.*

*Brinx Jones Brewing Company (Opening fall 2017)

They say that man's best friend is his dog, and in the case of Stephen Wozniak, that saying proves correct. After all, Steve named his craft brewery **Brinx Jones** after his own dog. Steve is a professional musician from Haddon Township who has played at many venues across the United States. As his interest in craft beer grew, he decided to return to his home state and start a craft brewery.

Settling on an impressive store front, a building that used to house Woolworths, Steve got busy turning a piece of history into an onsite craft brewery with character. The original tin ceiling from 1939 is still in place and adds a nostalgic feel to the space. Look for it as you take a seat at the sixty two foot long bar. The bar, too, is made from the past. Original Woolworth shelving was salvaged and now serves as the hub of the brewery.

Sixteen beers will eventually be flowing with taps serving up some flagship originals and rotating styles. IPAs, British Isle styles, Belgians, Wheats, and Steve's favorite *Irish Red*, a bready beer with a soft golden red color brewed from Maris Otter malt, will soon be swimming in your mouth. Don't be shy about trying them all; here there is a style of beer to fit every palate. When ordering a flight, check out the flight board. In keeping with the theme of using wood from the original building, you might find some fun graffiti scribbled on your board. Even back in the 1940s and 50s, Sally ♡ Jimmy.

Brinx Jones Brewing Company is situated in downtown Vineland. The expansive tasting room will also serve as an art gallery, with works of art from local artists on display and for sale.

Be sure to check their website or social media sites for opening news before you go. We can't wait to try their beers!

Important Information:

Address: 613 East Landis Ave Unit A, Vineland, NJ 08360

Guide to South Jersey Breweries

Phone: (856)405-6993

Website: www.brinxjones.com

Email: brinxjones@gmail.com

Days and hours: Check website for updates

To go: growlers

Events: Look for music, game nights (check social media)

Social media:

https://www.facebook.com/brinxjonesbrewing/

Twitter@brinxjones

-Photo courtesy of Brinx Jones Brewing Company

Handcrafted tables await your arrival at
Glasstown.

Glasstown Brewing Company

What's the most interesting thing you have ever done on a plane, excluding the mile-high club? How about writing a business plan on the five hour journey to your honeymoon destination? That's exactly what Jenifer and Paul Simmons did. And what a plan it was, as evidenced by their flourishing craft brewery, **Glasstown Brewing Company**, located in Millville, NJ.

After successfully brewing beer in college and impressing his friends enough with his product to take a leap into the craft brewing business, Paul enlisted the help of his wife, Jenifer, and opened up **Glasstown Brewing Company** on December 20,

2103, less than a year after they got married. Talk about a whirlwind first year of marital bliss!

Glasstown Brewing Company is located in Millville, NJ, a town famous for its glass manufacturing. In fact, **Glasstown** uses local glass. All the glasses used are products of Durand Glass Manufacturing located right in Millville, keeping the 'glass' in '**Glasstown**.'

Driving up to the brewery, you might notice something very special. Its location is smack in the middle of an old WWII airfield and surrounded by such nostalgia as army barracks, vintage airplanes, and even an old movie theater. You might be lucky and catch a plane take off or land in the newer part of the airport. The brewery occupies what used to be a garage, and it comes with plenty of parking and spectacular evening sunsets.

Glasstown Brewing Company doesn't only have a unique and interesting location, but it also offers exciting, thirst-quenching beers. This IPA -centric brewery uses the highest quality ingredients to create beers for everyone. Try the bestselling ***609***, a hoppy IPA with hints of citrus. Indulge in the much coveted ***Danky Kong***, an American IPA as playful as its name and fast becoming a **Glasstown** classic. This drinkable 7.2 % ABV has a familiar citrus nose and finish, and has enough hops to make it a potential barrel thrower. **Danky Jr.**, its formidable younger brother, carries a somewhat fruitier edge as a session

Guide to South Jersey Breweries

IPA. If you're not a seasoned beer drinker, just ask. The staff is educated and friendly and will help foster your beer palate.

  One thing you will notice here is the feeling of family and community. This brewery has become so popular with some patrons, that they've formed a quasi family with their *Glasstown Growler* group, spending time together, beer in hand, in what they term "group therapy." Fellowship over good beer has turned many a virtual stranger into lifelong friends. This expanding brewery will guarantee a good time, a brush with some notable history, and a full heart upon departure. Come.

Important Information:

Address: 10 Peterson St. Millville, NJ 08332

Phone: (856)327-7770

Website: www.glasstownbrewingcompany.com

Email: glasstownbrew@gmail.com

Days and hours: Thurs 3-9, Fri and Sat 12-9, Sun 12-7

To go: growlers, crowlers, cans, bottles

Events: First Friday music (check social media), adult Easter egg hunt, ornament hunt, various community charity events

Social media:

https://www.facebook.com/glasstownbrewingco

http://instagram.com/glasstownbrewing

Twitter@Glasstownbrew

Gloucester County

Gloucester County Beer Trail Map

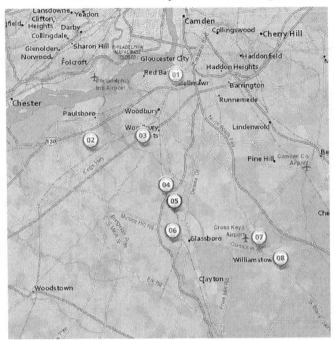

**1)Westville 2)Eight and Sand 3)Death of the Fox
4)Human Village 5)Kelly Green 6)Bonesaw
7)Cross Keys 8)13ᵗʰ Child**

Beer Trail One: Start at **Westville** (check that
they opened). *Taste beer.* Drive four minutes via
Broadway to Woodbury's **Eight and Sand**. *Taste beer.*
Drive eleven minutes via 295 S and then Berkley
Road to **Death of the Fox**. *Taste beer or drink coffee.*

Beer Trail Two: Start at **Human Village**. *Taste
beer.* Walk down two storefronts to **Kelly Green**.
Taste beer. Drive to **Bonesaw** (check if opened). *Taste*

beer. Drive thirteen minutes via Cross Keys Road then Main Street to **Cross Keys** (check if opened). *Taste beer.* Drive five minutes down Main street to **13th Child** (check that it opened) *Taste beer.*

What????

Sours are inoculated with bacteria. This sours the wort. But stop! Don't worry. The bacteria is killed off during the boiling process. There is no risk to you. Enjoy. Partake. You won't regret it.

*13th Child Brewery (opening fall 2017)

Anyone who lives in South Jersey, namely in the area of the Pine Barrens, has heard of the Jersey

Devil. The Jersey Devil is rumored to have been the 13th child of the Leeds family. Mother Leeds already had twelve children when she learned she was pregnant with the thirteenth. In anger and frustration, she cursed this pregnancy and soon a devil was born, complete with wings, hooves, and the head of a goat. There will be no need for cursing once you try the beer at **13th Child Brewery**. In fact, you might instead be singing an angelic, "Halleluiah!"

13th Child is the brainstorm of Steve MacNamara, Justin Seavernes, and Tom Nahf. The three came up with the name after a failed attempt to name their brewery *Blue Anchor*. After asking the public for help with the new name, an onslaught of Jersey Devil themed names poured in. Though not named specifically by the public, the Jersey Devil theme stuck, and **13th Child** was born.

Located on the point between Main Street and Blue Bell Road in downtown Williamstown, **13th Child Brewery** has all the charm and history a brewery can handle. Converted from a beautiful *First National Bank* dating back to 1906, **13th Child** boasts refinished wood floors and original mosaic tile. You'll be sipping beer in a historical, revitalized relic. How cool is that?

Though **13th Child** plans to keep to a Jersey Devil theme, there is nothing devilish about the beers, unless you want to call them devilishly good! **13th Child Brewery** brews beer while paying strict attention to detail, and their eight to ten taps will offer styles across the board. Rotating taps will deliver new creations regularly. Look for their seasonal beers. Local fruits and honey will add that special regional taste.

Stop in and say hello and enjoy some great craft beers. Look for parking on the street or in the large parking lot of the Pfeiffer Center, located across Blue Bell Rd to the right of the brewery.

Important Information:

Address: 345 South Main Street, Williamstown, NJ 08094

Phone: (856)776-8523

Website: www.blueanchorbrewing@gmail.com

Email: contact@13thchildbrewery.com

Days and hours: Check website or social media

To go: growlers

Events: Tastings, Main Street events, other (Check social media)

Social Media:

https://www.facebook.com/13th-Child-Brewery-1240773062632643/

https://instagram.com13thchild_brewing

Slugs like beer.

Can you blame them?

*Bonesaw Brewing Co (opening early 2018)

If you're hobnobbing in the Glassboro, Gloucester County area, take a ride by 570 Mullica Hill Road, also known as Route 322, to see if the doors are open to this exciting, new craft brewery. With a planned opening of early 2018, **Bonesaw Brewing Co** is a welcome addition to the landscape and to lovers of a good craft beer. Dreams have turned into reality with the construction of this beautiful brewery. **Bonesaw Brewing** will be brewing up some wonderful beers. Be sure to check their social media sites for more information.

Important Information:

Address: 570 Mullica Hill Road, Glassboro, NJ

Website: www.bonesawbrewing.com

Email: info@sawbonesbrewing.com

Days and hours: Check website

Social Media:

https://www.facebook.com/bonesawbrewing

https://www.instagram.com/bonesawbrewing/

Twitter@BonesawBrewing

Cross Keys Brewing Co awaits your arrival.

*Cross Keys Brewing Co (opening fall/winter 2017)

After searching for over two years to find the perfect location for their craft brewery, owners Alice and Alan Gorney and Evan and Tamika Fritz found a building big enough to fit their vision. A large tasting room of urban industrial style holds one hundred and forty people. What an awesome place for an event!

Artists by trade, Alice and Alan plan to incorporate their love of art into the venture. Look for rotating art by local artists to join the rotating taps of **Cross Keys Brewing Co.**

Cross Keys will offer a wide range of beers from IPAs to wheats to stouts, porters, sours, and farmhouse style saisons. Admire the creations of the artists while admiring the work of the brewers. A great beer in itself is a work of art.

 Cross Keys will make for a fun night out. They share the parking lot with an escape room. Imagine solving clues to escape a locked room after a pint of beer? What can be more fun than that?

 Cross Keys is looking to bring a bit of excitement and entertainment to Williamstown. Look for art events, yoga, music, and open mic nights. See their website or social media for updates.

 Williamstown has gained a gem in this craft brewery. Come and say hello. **Cross Keys Brewing Co** is not to be missed. Get ready to enjoy their large tasting room and great beer while playing a game of giant tumbling blocks. Cheers.

Important information:

Address: 1038 North Main Street, Williamstown, NJ 08094

Website: https://www.ckbcbeer.com/

Email: info@ckbcbeer.com

Days and hours: Check website

Social media:

https://www.facebook.com/ckbcbeer

https://www.instagram.com/ckbcbee

The study of beer is called
ZYTHOLOGY.
Good, we needed another z
word in the English language

Death of the Fox offers a comfortable   sitting area to sip coffee or beer.

Death of the Fox Brewing Company

Local brewer and avid history lover Chuck Garrity is onto something good. Chuck, president of **Death of the Fox Brewing Company** and his partners, Kathryn Garrity and Dan Natkin, have added a bit of flair to the growing area of Clarksboro. Their brewery, **Death of the Fox**, is unique in that it is the first in the state to be both a coffeehouse and a craft brewery. Yes, you can come early in the morning for a caffeinated pick me up, and then enjoy a cold beer in the afternoon or evening.

Upon entering the space with its high ceiling and urban edge decor, you notice something... a sense of comfort, much like the warm, cozy feeling of a hunter's lounge. This is exactly the feel they were going for. **Death of the Fox Brewing Company** pays tribute to the meeting house of the first fox hunting club in America, The Gloucester Fox Hunting Club, which dates back to the early 1700s and is located only a mile from the brewery. Many years ago, after a fox hunt, participants would head back to the tavern, also called Death of the Fox, to mingle and unwind. **Death of the Fox Brewing Company** succeeds in offering that same atmosphere. Warm, comfortable couches and low tables intermingle well with the handcrafted higher tables and bar, made from local wood. You'll take in the comforting smell of coffee, and you'll breathe a relaxing sigh.

But don't let the soothing smell of coffee fool you; this is still home to great beer with sixteen taps and an impressive list of beers, from traditional to more experimental. Their flagships include the crazily popular *Hazy Crazy Diamond*, a smooth but hoppy New England Style IPA and *No Grounds*, a Coffee Pale Ale which has been dry hopped with coffee beans from local coffee roaster Crescent Moon. Their *Stout Heard Around the World* is an award winner, a dark and chocolaty stout sure to please even the dark beer newbie.

Modeled after a German brewing system Speidels-braumeister, **Death of the Fox** is a ten barrel brewery which uses a single vessel system, or a BIP (brew in place), allowing for brewing three beers at one time. In fact, this system has helped appropriate a beer name, though somewhat unceremoniously. The two smaller tanks of the system can easily lift over three hundred pounds of mash mixture. But when it came to the bigger tank which holds eight to nine hundred pounds, upon hoisting up the tank with the lift, the top bar that holds the tank was unable to sustain the weight, and it bent almost in half. Luckily, the beer was saved by pumping it into the smaller tanks and the handle replaced with stronger steel, but not without christening the beer with its name, *Get Bent IPA*, which happens to be really delicious.

If you want a truly sensory experience, from the coffee smell, to the beer taste, to the creative music tickling your ears, come at once to this brewery. **Death of the Fox Brewing Company** is like a warm blanket; cozy, warm, and wonderful.

Important Information:

Address: 119 Berkley Road, Clarksboro, NJ 08020

Phone: (856)599-1655

Website: www.deathofthefoxbrewing.com

Email: dotfbrewmaster@comcast.net

Days and Hours: Mon-Tues 7am-2pm, Wed-Sat 7am-10pm, Sun 8am-6pm(beer tasting begins at noon)

To go: Crowlers

Events: Saturday Vinyl DJs, Soulful Sundays, Grateful

Sundays (Grateful Dead All Day)

Check social media site for live music featuring local and Philadelphia artists

Social Media:

www.facebook.com/deathofthefoxbrewing

www.instagram.com/deathofthefoxbrewingco

Twitter@DOTFBrewingCo

A saisonnier is a French farm worker. Years ago pale ales with lower ABVs were stored for drinking during the summer months and served to the workers who toiled in the fields. Saisons were born!

Beautiful outdoor area at Eight and Sand.

Eight and Sand Beer Co

What happens when you take a dilapidated, 4,600 square foot ex-pasta factory, unoccupied for over three years, and mix it with two young upstarts and a supporting dad? Answer: After a labor of love, the extraordinary delivery of a craft brewery called **Eight and Sand Beer Co**, focused on serving up classic European style beer!

After ten years of home brewing, Chris Burke teamed up with his childhood friend Chris Mazzone, and Chris' dad, Dom Mazzone, to start a brewery to help liven up the town of Woodbury, NJ. After purchasing the building on Evergreen Ave., the three got busy building their dreams. "Beer is proof that God wants us to be happy," Dom said one day to his son. Though this quote is often credited to Ben

Franklin, the original quote actually refers to grapes changing to wine as consistent proof of God's love. Beer? Wine? Didn't matter; it was enough of a push to start the now flourishing **Eight and Sand Beer Co**. The name comes from old railroad jargon, one wishing a train crew a safe ride.

Eight and Sand Beer Co uses a combination of American and European ingredients to create first-class beer. This ten barrel brewery is chock-full of choices with an average of seventeen beers on tap. With a focus on classic European style beer, there is something for everyone. Try the ***Monkey and the Engineer***, a Hefeweizen style, with its notes of banana, clove, and vanilla. Or perhaps you'd like something bolder like the creamy ***Bad Hombre***, a milk stout with just enough kick to make you wiggle in your seat. Not sure which of their many interesting beers to try? No problem, as "rails" of four 4oz pours are available for your drinking pleasure.

While you are enjoying the beer, be sure to check out the walls showcasing railroad memorabilia, and feel like a kid again sitting on one of the bright yellow bottle cap seats. In fact, while you are there, listen for the whistle of the train that passes three times a day just a few buildings down. The outdoor drinking area, complete with fire pit and games, is substantial, with plenty of space for a large gathering of friends or family.

Eight and Sand Beer Co is an energy efficient brewery, with an impressive sustainability plan, sending spent grain to local farmers, adding a solar array and even a flushless urinal. It might be worth going just to check that out!

Do yourself a favor and head to Woodbury's **Eight and Sand Beer Co**. The bright orange on the exterior of the building will pull you in, but the beer will make you stay.

Important Information:

Address: 1003 North Evergreen Ave., Woodbury, NJ 08096

Phone: (856)537-1339

Website: www.eightandsandbeer.com

Email: info@eightandsandbeer.com

Days and Hours: Thurs 5-10, Fri 5-10, Sat 12-10, Sun 12-7

To go: growlers, 22 oz bottles, sixtels, kegs

Events: Many, check facebook

Social Media:
https://www.facebook.com/eightandsandbeer/

https://www.instagram.com/eightsandbeer/

Twitter@EightSandBeer

The beautiful mural painted by Michele
Peraino at Human Village.

Human Village Brewing Co

Three things apparent at **Human Village Brewing Co:** love of art, music, and balanced beer. Visually, the brewery is unique; you might think you are in a music museum complete with old LP records on the wall, nostalgic photos of musicians, and a beautiful music themed mural created by the talented Michele Peraino. The impressive mural of John Coltrane playing the song 'Blue Train' on his alto saxophone confirms this craft brewery is one filled with melody in the form of tunes, beer, and friendship.

Homebrewers for over six years, owners Megan and Richard Myers, transformed Pitman's beloved landmark, the *Bus Stop Music Café*, into the thriving nanobrewery, **Human Village Brewing Co**. Setting up shop in Pitman was an easy decision for Megan and Richard. The quaint town with lots of charm and character mirrored their own principles and those of the brewery: values of community and hospitality. In fact, the **Human Village** name comes from the time when beer was brewed to serve the social function of bringing community together to converse and relax. That is exactly what you will discover here.

Human Village Brewing Co has introduced styles and flavors of beers that have been lacking in the market. The handcrafted, well-balanced beer is created in small quantities, one batch at a time, and still stirred as beer was stirred years ago, with a wooden mash paddle. You might not want to misbehave here, unless that paddle has been put away!

Though focused on Continental European style beers, **Human Village** offers an impressive selection for a small brewery. With an average of nine beers on tap, you are sure to find one to suit your palate. The flagship ***Beers and the Bees*** golden ale is popular and made with local honey. Other favorites include the black IPA , ***Fade to Black,*** and IPA, ***Abby Road***. Check out their sours, too. They are concurrently pleasant and sure to set off a delightful earthquake in your soul. Can't make up your mind? Try a flight of four 4 oz pours.

Human Village is becoming a destination not only for the beer, but also for its open mic nights currently held every Thursday. In keeping with the *Bus Stop*

Music Café tradition, the open mic nights are a big hit, and all aspiring performers are welcome to show off their talents.

Stop by; ask questions about the beer; try them all. Megan and Richard are looking forward to seeing you! The beer is awaiting your arrival.

Important Information:

Address: 148 South Broadway, Pitman, NJ 08071

Phone: (856)556-0639

Website: https://www.humanvillagebrewingco.com

Email: villager@humanvillagebrewingco.com

Days and hours: Thurs-Fri 5-10, Sat 3-10

To go: growlers

Events: Thursday open mic, live music (see social media)

Social media:

www.facebook.com/humanvillagebrewingco

http://instagram.com/humanbrewing

Twitter@HumanBrewing

Justin is ready to serve you at Kelly Green.

Kelly Green Brewing Co

A few years ago, if you strolled through the quaint Gloucester County town of Pitman, NJ, you'd have noticed there was neither a pint of beer to be sold nor a glass of wine to be bought. The historically dry town stayed sleepily dehydrated until a bold force of young visionaries arrived with a plan to bring some moisture to the air. Though still considered a dry town (but watch out; that might soon change with a liquor license soon to be put up for bid), Pitman now has an awesome watering hole thanks to **Kelly Green Brewing Co.**

Owners Justin Fleming, David Domanski, and Mike

Tacconelli, have turned an old storefront office building into a small, but thriving, Eagles themed nanobrewery with an Irish twist. Note the green walls and framed Eagles Jersey intermingling with Irish style tiles and an awesome **Kelly Green** emblem. Take a seat at the hand crafted bar or the homemade benches and tables. You are sure to strike up a conversation with someone who could tell you a bit about the interesting history of this small town with a big heart, originally founded as a Methodist camp meeting; and as you sip your beer, bask in the knowledge that you are sipping a beer in a place with the distinction of being the first craft brewery opened in a dry town, in the state of NJ.

Kelly Green Brewing Co. was a grateful leap from the years of home brewing Justin did with his friend David. After suffering a torn shoulder and having time to ruminate on what's important in life, Justin decided that leaving a job he disliked and taking a risk to do something he enjoyed, was a small price to pay for being happy. Being a Pitmanite, Pitman was a natural fit, and Kelly Green opened its doors in November of 2016. Pitman residents and Kelly Green guests have been good to these brewers. They are already looking to expand in the near future.

This craft brewery has an average of eight to ten beers on tap, with the ***Off Broadway IPA,*** their flagship signature and ***End Grain Coffee Porter***, a creamy porter made with Pitman's *End Grain* coffee, being popular with the guests.

Kelly Green is small in size but large in popularity. It is not unusual to see long lines of beer lovers outside the door waiting to get their hands on bottle releases of new beers like barrel aged saisons, French farmhouse style fermented with wild strains of yeast and sour characteristics. Many of these are traded nationally.

Stop by after a hot day of shopping downtown and see what all the fuss is about. You'll be glad you did.

Important Information:

Address: 154 South Broadway, Pitman, NJ 08071

Phone: (856)270-2876

Website: kellygreenbrewing.com

Email: kellybrewingco@gmail.com

Days and hours: Wed-Thurs 5-10, Fri 3-10, Sat 12-10, Sun 12-6

To go: growlers, crowlers (soon...ask), bottle releases

Events: Eagles game Monday Night Football, Saturday live music (check social media)

Social Media:

http://facebook.com/kellygreenbrewingco

http://instagram.com/kellygreenbrewingcom

The gang at Westville can't wait to meet you!

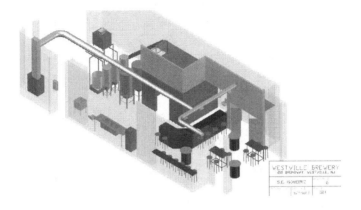

*Westville Brewery (opening early 2018)

The little town of Westville will soon have an awesome craft brewery ready to serve up really good beer. Located along the main business area in Westville, **Westville Brewery** will be making its debut in early 2018. Owners Mike Gordy, Pam Gordy, John Metz, and Chuck Eckert, have joined forces and beer brewing knowledge to craft some great brews ready for your drinking pleasure. This nanobrewery will be a welcome addition to downtown, bringing foot traffic and pints of fun to the area.

With six to eight beers on tap, Mike explains there will be something to please every palate. His *Pipe Wrench Porter* is a must try. Mike has been perfecting his recipe for *Pipe Wrench Porter* for years, and he is looking forward to serving it to you.

The tasting room of this craft brewery pays homage to the firehouse it used to be. Firehouse red dons the walls, and historical thematic photos of local firehouses and firefighters will soon be up.

Brewing beer is not always easy. Just ask Pam who is learning the ropes from her veteran partners. While brewing her very first batch, the full five gallon pot was too heavy for the ceramic top stove. After hearing a large cracking sound, she noticed a large crack in her burner. She switched burners and continued on. Soon, another large crack was heard. She knew the other burner had fractured as well, but with the perseverance of a seasoned brewer, she continued boiling anyway and made a fine beer. Her partners joke that it was a five hundred dollar price tag for a five gallon batch of beer. Yes, she needed a new stove after that. But practice makes perfect, and the beer is as close to perfect as you can get.

Westville Brewery invites you to meet them at the clock. Look for the beautiful clock in downtown Westville. The brewery is just to the right and behind the clock. After all, it's always five o'clock somewhere. Mike, Pam, John, and Chuck are looking forward to meeting you and serving you a beer of your taste, whether a porter, ale, saison, or other. They can't wait to meet you!

Guide to South Jersey Breweries

Important Information:

Address: 201 Broadway, Westville, NJ 08093

Website: westvillebrewery.com

Email: westvillebrewery@gmail.com

Days and hours: Check website

To go: growlers

Events: Look for paint nights and open mic (see website and social media)

Social Media:

https://www.facebook.com/westvillebrewery/

-Graphic courtesy of Westville Brewery

Hundreds of years ago, Roggenbier was outlawed for a time. This beer, made from 50% rye malt, was brewed in Germany. But during a life threatening famine, people used the malt to brew beer instead of using it to make life saving food such as bread. Can you see why it was outlawed?

Brew Pubs:

Iron Hill Maple Shade and Voorhees:

This brew pub, named to honor those who fought on Iron Hill during the Revolutionary War, recently celebrated twenty years in business. The beers are brewed on site, and the food ranges from a slew of great appetizers to burgers, salads, and plentiful entrees.

Maple Shade

124 East Kings Highway, Maple Shade, NJ

Phone: (856)273-0300

Voorhees:

13107 Town Center Blvd, Voorhees, NJ 08043

Phone: (856)545-9009

Tun Tavern Atlantic City:

Tun Tavern is named for the tavern Samuel Carpenter built in 1683 in Philadelphia. Samuel knew that by building over a spring in which the purest water flowed, great beer could be brewed. Tun Tavern continues the tradition of brewing excellent beer. They offer a full menu from appetizers, to soups and salads, burgers, and more.

Address: 2 Convention Blvd, Atlantic City, NJ 08401

Phone: (609)347-7800

Avalon Brew Pub:

This beachfront microbrewery offers beer brewed on-site, but also a full cocktail menu and great food.

Address: 79th Street & the Beach, Avalon, NJ 08202

Phone: (609)967-2116

Coming soon:

Mudhen Brewing Company and Smokehouse:

This brewery, named for the first passenger train in Wildwood, will offer craft beer and smokehouse style food.

Address: 127 W Rio Grande, Wildwood, NJ 08260

More Beer Trails: Inter-county (*means check if opened yet)

- *Common Sense* to *Third State* to *Double Nickel* to *Eclipse*

- *Village Idiot* to *Spellbound* to *Zed's* to *Nale House* to *Lower Forge*

- *Berlin* to *Atco* to *Three 3's* to *Tomfoolery* to *Vinyl**

- *Brinx Jones** to *Glasstown* to *Ludlam Island* to *Slack Tide*

- *Devil's Creek* to *Tonewood* to *Red, White and Brew** to *Eight and Sand* to *Death of the Fox*

- *Cross Keys* to 13th Child* to Black Horse* to Garden State to Hidden Sands*

- *Westville to Bonesaw* to Kelly Green to Human Village to Lunacy to King's Road**

- *Double Nickel to Eclipse to Forgotten Boardwalk to Flying Fish*

- *Tuckahoe to Ludlam to Slacktide*

Brewery visit check off sheet with space for notes

☐ **7 Mile**

☐ **13th Child**

☐ **Atco**

☐ **Berlin**

☐ **Black Horse**

☐ **Bonesaw**

- [ ] **Brinx Jones**

- [ ] **Bucket Brigade**

- [ ] **Cape May**

- [ ] **Cold Springs**

- [ ] **Common Sense**

- [ ] **Cross Keys**

- [ ] **Death of the Fox**

☐ **Devil's Creek**

☐ **Double Nickel**

☐ **Eclipse**

☐ **Eight and Sand**

☐ **Forgotten Boardwalk**

☐ **Flying Fish**

☐ **Garden State**

☐ **Glasstown**

☐ **Hidden Sands**

☐ **Human Village**

☐ **Kelly Green**

☐ **King's Road**

☐ **Lower Forge**

☐ **Ludlam Island**

- ☐ **Lunacy**

- ☐ **Nale House**

- ☐ **Red, White, and Brew**

- ☐ **Slack Tide**

- ☐ **Spellbound**

- ☐ **Third State**

- ☐ **Three 3's**

- [ ] **Tomfoolery**

- [ ] **Tonewood**

- [ ] **Tuckahoe**

- [ ] **Village Idiot**

- [ ] **Vinyl**

- [ ] **Westville**

- [ ] **Zed's**

A Note from *Visit South Jersey*

In a state as packed with people as it is with things to see, the counties that stretch from the South Jersey suburbs across the Delaware from Philadelphia to the shores of the Delaware Bay radiate natural beauty, small-town charm, and one-of-a-kind experiences that mean you don't have to seek out a big city to enjoy.

Today, the culture that anchors some of the oldest settled communities in America supports contemporary, five-star dining; unique shopping districts; and a bountiful wine region fast earning a reputation for its remarkable quality and taste.

South Jersey has also benefited from the nationwide boom in craft brewery, with standbys like Yuengling, the oldest brewery in America, expanding their profiles at tap houses to compete with regional products. More than ever, the area beer experience is as much a local as a cosmopolitan one, with signature products on display sometimes mere miles from their bottling source.

Craft-batch brewery startups are also growing rapidly in South Jersey, with a handful of local beer-makers joining in the revolution at their own facilities throughout the area. Visiting these spaces has become a must for beer lovers who want to experience the process first-hand. Self-guided tours culminate in tasting rooms where guests can chat up brewmasters and sample the varieties of brews.

Here in South Jersey, the lively attractions that begin at the celebrated Jersey Shore continue inland, following the greenery from which the Garden State draws its name. Throughout those cranberry bogs and blueberry fields, acres of Jersey corn and greenhouses brimming with heirloom tomatoes, an efficient network of transit options provides a quick connection from one activity to the next, by rail, highway, or scenic county road.

About Visit South Jersey - Visit South Jersey (VSJ) is the official Destination Marketing Organization for Burlington, Camden, Gloucester and Salem counties, and the Outer Coast Plain Wine Region in South Jersey. Working with thousands of tourism stakeholders, VSJ promotes travel to the region by creating and packaging tourism product, and marketing South Jersey as a destination. VSJ is a non-profit organization supported in part by a grant from the New Jersey Department of State, Division of Travel and Tourism. For more information about travel to South Jersey, or for a copy of the Visitor's Guide, please visit visitsouthjersey.com and be sure to check out the Visit South Jersey free app via your cellphone app provider.

Guide to South Jersey Breweries

Facebook: Visit South Jersey
Twitter: @VisitSJersey
Instagram: @Visit_South_Jersey

Hashtags:
#VisitSouthJersey
#SouthJersey
#VSJ
#WineWednesday
#TuesdayBrewsday
#craftsouthjersey

About the author:

Maureen Fitzpatrick is a teacher, writer, mom, and craft beer lover. She has written a poetry book and has been a guest writer in various poetry books and publications. She lives with her family in Gloucester County, NJ.

For inquiries:
beertrailbook@gmail.com

www.twintitianpress.com

https://www.facebook.com/Guide-to-New-Jersey-Craft-Breweries-South-Jersey-Edition-132833574013272/

Follow on instagram@beertrailbooksouthjersey

About the photographer:

Joan's love for photography started when she was young. She studied black and white photography and portraiture, as well as Digital Photography and computer design courses at Gloucester County College (now Rowan College Gloucester County), and recently completed an online course, "Seeing through Photographs" by The Museum of Modern Art. Her love for photography and capturing moments that make great photography is her passion. She resides in Pitman with her son Andrew.

For inquiries:

www.intriguedbyimages.com

Guide to South Jersey Breweries

Available at amazon.com
barnesandnoble.com
Selective Barnes and Noble Stores
Independent retailers

For more fun things to do in South Jersey, go to

visitsouthjersey.com

77411991R00135

Made in the USA
Columbia, SC
20 September 2017